ROUTLEDGE LIBRARY EDITIONS:
JAPAN

BANKING POLICY IN JAPAN

BANKING POLICY IN JAPAN
American Efforts at Reform During the Occupation

WILLIAM M. TSUTSUI

Volume 19

Routledge
Taylor & Francis Group

LONDON AND NEW YORK

First published in 1988

This edition first published in 2011
by Routledge
2 Park Square, Milton Park, Abingdon, Oxon, OX14 4RN

Simultaneously published in the USA and Canada
by Routledge
711 Third Avenue, New York, NY 10017

Routledge is an imprint of the Taylor & Francis Group, an informa business

© 1988 William M. Tsutsui

First issued in paperback 2013

British Library Cataloguing in Publication Data
A catalogue record for this book is available from the British Library

ISBN 13: 978-0-415-58525-5 (hbk)

ISBN 13: 978-0-415-85269-2 (pbk)

Publisher's Note
The publisher has gone to great lengths to ensure the quality of this reprint but
points out that some imperfections in the original copies may be apparent.

Disclaimer
The publisher has made every effort to trace copyright holders and would
welcome correspondence from those they have been unable to trace.

BANKING POLICY IN JAPAN

American efforts at reform during the Occupation

WILLIAM M. TSUTSUI

ROUTLEDGE
London and New York

First published in 1988 by
Routledge
11 New Fetter Lane, London EC4P 4EE

Published in the USA by
Routledge
in association with Routledge, Chapman and Hall, Inc.
29 West 35th Street, New York NY 10001

Printed in Great Britain by
Billing & Sons Ltd, Worcester

British Library Cataloguing in Publication Data

Tsutsui, William M.
    Banking policy in Japan: American efforts
    at reform during the occupation.
    1. Japan. Banking. Reform. Role of United
    States, 1945–1952
    I. Title
    332.1′0952
ISBN: 0-415-00003-3

Library of Congress Cataloging-in-Publication Data
ISBN: 0-415-00003-3

For my father

Contents

Contents

General Editor's Preface

Almost imperceptibly during the 1980s, Japan has become 'hot news'. The successes of the Japanese economy and the resourcefulness of her people have long been appreciated abroad. What is new is an awareness of her increasing impact on the outside world. This tends to produce painful adjustment and uncomfortable reactions. It also often leads to stereotypes and arguments based on outdated or ill-informed ideas.

The Nissan Institute/Routledge Japanese Studies Series (previously the Nissan Institute/Croom Helm Japanese Studies Series) seeks to foster an informed and balanced — but not uncritical — understanding of Japan. One aim of the series is to show the depth and variety of Japanese institutions, practices and ideas. Another is, by using comparison, to see what lessons, positive and negative, can be drawn for other countries. There are many aspects of Japan which are little known outside that country but which deserve to be better understood.

Between 1945 and 1952 Japan underwent a radical and wide-ranging reordering of her political, economic and social institutions administered by the Allied (largely American) Occupation. Many of the reforms brought about by the Occupation, such as the democratic 'peace' Constitution, the changes in the status of the emperor, the land reform, reform of the social code and so on, are well known. What is less well known, because hitherto little researched, are American attempts to reform the banking system. Mr Tsutsui argues that for reasons in part of Occupation politics, the Americans essentially failed to reform the banking system. The norms of the existing system, far removed from those which American bankers regarded as normal or desirable, were largely preserved. Yet this was to have a profound and positive impact upon the economic transformation of Japan in subsequent years.

J.A.A. Stockwin
Director, Nissan Institute of Japanese Studies, University of
Oxford

Acknowledgements

This book grew out of a Master of Letters thesis submitted to the University of Oxford in 1987. My postgraduate studies would have been impossible without the financial support so generously given by the Marshall Aid Commemoration Commission. Additional funding was provided by Corpus Christi College, which awarded me a travel grant to help defray the costs of research in the United States.

I would like to extend my deep appreciation to Professor J.A.A. Stockwin, who gave freely of his time, intellect and experience as my academic supervisor at Oxford. Dr Jennifer Corbett and Sir Alec Cairncross, who served as the examiners of my thesis, contributed valuable criticisms and suggestions for further investigation. Mr Richard Finn, formerly of the Center for International Affairs at Harvard University, deserves special thanks for providing me with unpublished material, personal contacts and continuous encouragement in my work. I am also indebted to Mr Tristan Beplat and Suzuki Gengo for sharing their personal recollections of the Occupation with me. My archival research was greatly facilitated by the assistance given by the staffs of the Washington National Records Center in Suitland, Maryland and the Burton Historical Collection of the Detroit Public Library. Finally, I would like to thank my mother, whose tolerance and enthusiasm made the going easier, and Marjorie Swann, for whose constant support and tireless proof-reading I am very grateful indeed.

Abbreviations Used in the Text

DRB   Deconcentration Review Board

ESB   Economic Stabilization Board

ESS   Economic and Scientific Section

ESS–A/C   Antitrust and Cartels Division, ESS

ESS-FI   Finance Division, ESS

FEC   Far Eastern Commission

HCLC   Holding Company Liquidation Commission

JCS   Joint Chiefs of Staff

JDB   Japan Development Bank

M&B   Money and Banking Branch, ESS-FI

RFB   Reconstruction Finance Bank

SCAP   Supreme Commander for the Allied Powers
(used to refer both to General MacArthur individually and to the American bureaucracy in Occupied Japan as a whole)

SCAPIN   SCAP Instruction
(Occupation directive to the Japanese Government)

SWNCC   State-War-Navy Coordinating Committee

Introduction

The work of the American Occupation of Japan (1945–52) has been examined from many perspectives, yet remains today only imperfectly understood. In the decades since the San Francisco Peace Treaty, there has been a tendency in the West, particularly in the United States, to romanticise and exaggerate the importance of the American tenure in Japan. The view that the Occupation period stands as a great watershed in the course of Japanese history, indeed comparable only to the Meiji Restoration in breadth and depth, has been widely disseminated and accepted. Many commentators, most notably former Occupation bureaucrats, have characterised the 'American interlude' as Japan's second 'opening', with MacArthur, like Perry before him, ushering in a flood of superior occidental ways which would eventually transform the whole of Japanese society. In recent years, great pains have been taken to link the Occupation's work with the economic 'miracle', an attempt, in effect, to trace the origins of Japan's postwar success to the policy and patronage of the SCAP administration. In retrospect, the Occupation has assumed semi-mythical proportions as a supposed vindication of American idealism and know-how, responsible in large part for shaping Japan into a prosperous, peaceful and democratic nation.

While defeat and occupation were certainly a crucial turning-point in Japan's modern development, the extent of change was not so great and the US contribution not so uniformly positive as some understandably biased American observers may have maintained. The record of Japan's economic success and political stability since 1952 has tended to obscure the internal weaknesses of the Occupation, the flaws in its policies and its numerous failures. As even the most superficial scrutiny will reveal, the history of the Occupation and its legacy in Japan cannot be easily detailed, neatly analysed or readily deemed an uncomplicated triumph of the American way.

Institutional reform on 'democratic' models was the focus of SCAP activity, yet the American accomplishments were uneven, with conspicuous failures as well as striking successes. While, for example, Japanese landholding patterns were fundamentally, permanently and admirably changed by the occupiers, many areas of society emerged little affected by direct American reform. The banking system was one of these, a critical sector of the economy not substantially altered by the American administration. The situation in banking was curious, as the historical importance and central economic role of finance seemed to make it an obvious target for SCAP reform — yet the Japanese banking system eluded restructuring under the antitrust initiatives, experienced only superficial legal reorganisation and, in general, was not subjected to the full intensity of American democratisation efforts. In the end, the financial sector appears to have been one of the most significant Japanese institutions (second only, perhaps, to the government bureaucracy) not to be caught in the flood of Occupation reformism.

Nevertheless, the Americans did not simply overlook reform of the Japanese financial system or purposefully omit it from their otherwise far-reaching democratisation programmes. Indeed, SCAP showed a decided commitment to the transformation of Japanese banking: exploring, planning and actively pursuing ambitious reform initiatives throughout the Occupation's tenure. Antitrust campaigners sought 'economic democracy' through forced deconcentration of the banking structure; legal experts offered comprehensive proposals for legislative revision; even Financial Advisor Joseph Dodge, often characterised as an arch-conservative and opponent of institutional reform, had a definite agenda for the 'Americanisation' of Japanese banking. Ultimately, however, the Occupation's various attempts at financial reform all ended in frustration, allowing for the maintenance of the *status quo* in banking and the continuance of the established arrangements which the Americans found 'undemocratic' and untenable.

The significance of the Americans' failure in banking policy has been noted by both economists and scholars of the Occupation. Some observers have considered banking reform the most serious omission from the US economic programme, a critical missing link in the chain of democratisation, which allowed for the survival of an oligopolistic, inequitable and economically inefficient financial system in Japan. Nevertheless, many commentators have also maintained that Japan's 'miracle' economy would have been severely handicapped by the realisation of American plans for financial change and that failure was therefore fortuitous, as the Japanese banking system which emerged, unreformed, from the years of Occupation proved eminently suited to the promotion of rapid economic growth. In short, the collapse of American financial reform efforts has been seen to have undermined the evolution of a fully 'democratic', and yet underlain the development of a highly successful one in postwar Japan.

Although the significance of the omission of banking from the American programme has been widely acknowledged, the Occupation initiatives have not been intensively researched nor have the reasons why finance remained unscathed been rigorously examined by Western scholars. The tendency in much of the literature on Occupation economic policy has been to ascribe failure in reform to forces external to the SCAP bureaucracy. Both ex-occupationaires and 'Cold War' historians, who have provided the bulk of literature on the Occupation, have preferred to seek reasons for the weaknesses of SCAP reform in the outside influences of Japanese intractability and Washington's geo-political strategising. Such an approach, however, seems to discount the importance of the SCAP bureaucracy and Joseph Dodge on the formulation and implementation of American policy in Japan. Indeed, while indigenous resistance and the 'reverse course' were of indisputable significance to the course of the entire Occupation mission, a close analysis reveals that such external factors cannot fully — or entirely accurately — account for the experience in financial reform. This study suggests that the progress of change in Occupied Japan was hindered as much, if not more, by conditions within SCAP — particularly bureaucratic infighting, deficient planning, a compartmentalised organisation and a generally rigid, self-righteous orientation — than by influences from outside MacArthur's domain.

The aim of this work is to document the Occupation's unsuccessful initiatives in banking reform and to provide an answer to the fundamental question of why the Americans did not manage to accomplish significant change in Japanese finance. The goal here is neither to present a full history of Japanese finance from 1945 to 1952, nor to offer a thorough economic examination of banking development during the American stewardship; rather, the objective is to investigate the nature of Occupation reformism and economic policy-making through the close analysis of one strand of the American 'democratisation' effort in Japan. In short, by looking microscopically at SCAP's intentions in financial reform, the process through which US banking policy was determined and the conditions under which the American initiatives failed, this study seeks to challenge — and hopefully somewhat muddy — a few of the simplistic interpretations and conventional assumptions which characterise much of the existing work on Occupation economic policy.

Chapter 1 provides an overview of the development of Japanese banking prior to the Occupation, establishing the historical background to the American reform programmes. SCAP's initial efforts are considered in Chapter 2, which describes the 'demilitarisation' of the financial system, the occupiers' apparently most successful (though in essence superficial) work in banking policy. Chapter 3 examines the 'trust busters'' proposal to democratise the Japanese banking structure by forced deconcentration, the Americans' most ambitious, idealistic (and economically impracticable) plan for financial reform. Chapter 4 investigates a rival scheme for democratisation — based on extensive legal revision — which was presented as a viable, constructive alternative to antitrust 'atomisation'. As Chapter 5 details, the last US attempt at reform — Dodge's plan for indirectly 'Americanising' Japanese finance — was much different in design and approach from the previous SCAP efforts, yet yielded equally disappointing results. Chapter 6, finally, presents an overview of the American failure in banking reform and a consideration of its consequences for the long-term development of the Japanese financial system.

1

Background to Reform: The Development of Japanese Banking, 1868–1945

The Japanese banking system which the American occupiers encountered in 1945 was highly developed and well established, not unlike its Western counterparts in essential respects, and yet quite obviously unique as a whole. While in institutional arrangements and basic functions Japan's financial world showed significant similarities to the American and European systems which had originally served as its models, much seemed alien to MacArthur's reformers, from the pattern of corporate finance to investment practices, from the legal structure to the fundamental economic philosophy of Japanese bankers, industrialists and civil servants. Perhaps not surprisingly, it was the singular characteristics of Japanese banking, those aspects unfamiliar and sometimes incomprehensible to the occupiers, that were to become the focus of American criticism and the target of reform efforts. An understanding of what the Americans considered the 'peculiarities' of Japanese banking, as well as an appreciation of the general nature of the system, is thus necessary as basic background to an analysis of the financial programmes of the Occupation.

Modern banking was introduced into Japan during the Meiji period (1868–1912) under the government's assertive policy of importing Western practices and organisational forms to support rapid industrialisation. The Japanese had faith in the efficiency of institutional models from the West, yet were flexible in the transfer and subsequent integration of foreign methods into the existing society. Thus the Japanese financial system did not develop as a mere clone of contemporary American and European arrangements but rather evolved under the influence of indigenous traditions, conditions and requirements. The long and often turbulent process of importation and adjustment ultimately produced the distinctive 'hybrid' system of banking which the occupiers encountered after the Pacific War.

The evolution of Japanese banking was shaped by innumerable forces: the nation's geography, patterns of government finance, the course of economic growth and trends in overseas trade, to note but a few. Several factors stand out, however, as being particularly significant, fundamental influences on the pre-1945 development of Japanese finance. First was a general weakness of domestic capital, a condition which derived from Japan's agrarian, pre-industrial heritage, but which continued well into the years of rapid economic progress. Secondly, a consistently high demand for credit, created by the brisk pace of industrialisation, had profound effects on the development of banking, corporate finance and industrial organisation. Lastly, the rise of militarism and the demands of a wartime economy became pervasive influences upon the growth and adjustment of the financial system after 1930. These were, in short, the basic pressures which forced deviation from the highly developed banking structures, established patterns of finance and conventional standards of operation which prevailed in the West, were provided as ideals for Japan, and yet proved not entirely suited to the unique local conditions.

The first decades of modern banking in Japan were a period of experimentation and seemingly constant flux in the structure of private-sector financial institutions. Although some bank-like organisations had existed prior to the Restoration of 1868, the Meiji leadership considered the formation of entirely new institutions based on Western models the most expedient means of effecting rapid financial modernisation. In banking, as in many other areas of economic innovation, the Meiji government took the lead in importing Western structures and practices but generally left the operation and internal development of the new system to private initiative — a pattern which Hugh Patrick termed 'governmental encouragement and entrepreneurial response'.[1]

The government initially adopted the contemporary American financial system as the model for Japan, and in 1872 put forward regulations allowing for the establishment of currency-issuing 'national' banks. The American-styled institutions, which were founded by private capital, did not prove a success, however, even after extensive reform of the system in 1876, as they remained dependent on government assistance and pursued an injudicious policy of issuing bank notes. Under Finance Minister Count Matsukata Masayoshi, the central authorities recognised the weaknesses of the 'national' bank arrangements and, apparently content to pursue a process of 'trial and error', sought a major reorganisation with the European system of finance as the new ideal. Hence, in 1882, to 'act as the center for national finance and help harmonize the activities of banks all across the country',[2] the Bank of Japan (patterned by Matsukata on the central bank of Belgium) was founded and vested with the exclusive right to issue currency. The structure of commercial banking was reformed under the Bank Act of 1890, which established a single new class of financial institution — the 'ordinary' banks — and set out a concise, unified code of rules to regulate the foundation, operation and administration of such organisations. By the turn of the century, when the transition to European forms was complete, national finance had been stabilised, the currency difficulties had been alleviated and the basis for a viable commercial banking structure was in place.

While the Meiji government showed considerable interest in establishing a solid, permanent financial structure, it exhibited considerably less concern about the internal operations of the private banks. English commercial banking, the most highly developed of the day, was widely held as an ideal for the operation of Japanese institutions,[3] but Western standards of practice were neither legislated by the government nor rigorously adhered to by bankers themselves. The 1890 Bank Act, for example, set no minimum capitalisation for financial institutions, put no restrictions on the outside business activities of banks and, as revised in 1895, established no statutory limits on advances to a single customer.[4] Without strict legal regulations, Japanese bankers, who did not innately espouse the re'ຸtively conservative, safety-minded attitudes of their Western coຸ.terparts, were not particularly inclined to maintain the financial practices held as sound and essential in Britain or the United States.

Not surprisingly, commercial banking was often in a precarious financial position during the Meiji period and beyond. Under the 1890 regulations, the number of 'ordinary' banks increased rapidly, peaking in 1901 at a total of 1,867 institutions. The vast majority of these were poorly-capitalised unit banks (though branching was not legally forbidden or even regulated by the government) and the average size was very small.[5] Almost none of the banks was competently managed by contemporary Western standards, as techniques of accounting and portfolio analysis were relatively slow to develop. Loan practices were often patently unsound as banks engaged in speculative advances, made extensive loans to directors and frequently concentrated their lending on one customer.[6] At the very extreme, 'organ' banks — institutions founded or managed solely to provide funds for a single client — were not uncommon in Japan prior to World War I.[7] Such banks were never entirely stable, as the young Japanese

3

economy was volatile and crises were frequent, causing difficulties for commercial and industrial firms which could, in turn, put extreme pressure on the banks which were closely tied to them.

In addition to the common lack of diversification in loan portfolios, the Meiji banks were generally aggressive in their credit practices and tended to extend loans beyond their financial capacity. The term 'overloan' has been widely used in studies of Japanese banking to refer to the condition where financial institutions (individually or collectively) have allowed advances to exceed deposits.[8] Such a situation has historically been rare in the West, but was common in Meiji Japan, at least until the turn of the century. The private sector's demand for credit was seemingly infinite — funds for expansion in booms, advances to cover shortfalls in recessions — and the Meiji banks tried to be solicitous, even if this required the compromise of sound banking practice. The long-term 'overloan' observed in Japan was only possible because of a permissive official attitude, the government apparently believing that financial expansion would promote rapid industrial development. Thus, 'ordinary' banks which encountered liquidity problems arising from aggressive lending policies were given easy accommodation by the Bank of Japan, providing a financial lifeline of discounts and direct loans which sustained many over-extended institutions during the Meiji period.[9]

Despite their frequent internal difficulties, the Japanese banks were called upon to play a major role in the financing of development. Commercial and industrial firms were reliant on external funding, as retained earnings were seldom sufficient to cover the financial needs of rapid economic growth. From the beginnings of industrialisation in the Meiji period, corporate finance in Japan has been predominantly 'indirect', that is, firms have tended to raise investment funds from financial intermediaries (especially banks) rather than by obtaining the required capital 'directly' through the sale of equities to individual savers. While Japanese industrial concerns were typically founded on the joint-stock form of organisation and stock exchanges had been established as early as 1878, firms found acquiring investment funds through bank credit easier and more dependable than through the issuance of securities. The emission of stock and corporate bonds became an increasingly important means of raising capital as the Japanese economy expanded during the first decades of this century, but the commercial banks, rather than individual investors, were responsible for taking up or indirectly financing the purchase of the majority of these new issues.[10] Individual shareholding was uncommon and the underdeveloped stock markets remained forums for speculation, as Japanese savers clearly preferred to entrust their money to the relatively secure financial institutions.[11]

The Japanese banks, called upon by business to provide the majority of investment funds, thus did not develop as purely commercial institutions. In striking contrast to the English model, the Japanese adopted what one author termed the 'department store method of banking'.[12] Rather than concentrating on the discounting of commercial bills, as the London clearing banks traditionally have, the Japanese institutions took on a wide range of financial activities — like the 'universal' banks of Central Europe — providing long-term loans for fixed investment and subscribing to corporate securities in addition to engaging in short-term commercial financing.[13] The extent of long-term lending by Japan's nominally commercial banks has proven hard to quantify, but statistics from the Meiji and the 1920s suggest that the 'ordinary' banks were heavily committed to such investment.[14] The practice of granting long-term credit, though apparently conducive to rapid industrial growth,[15] contributed to the critical interdependence of banks and their corporate clients, thus increasing the vulnerability of finance in Japan's unsettled economy.

Although certain generalisations can be made regarding the early Japanese commercial banks, there was certainly notable diversity amongst them. Most obviously (and significantly in the long term), during the first decades of this century a class of distinctive institutions emerged from the mass of small, unevenly managed and unstable 'ordinary' banks as the virtually unrivalled leaders of Japanese finance. These were the banks associated with the *zaibatsu*, Japan's great 'financial cliques', which were to become a dominant force not just in the world of banking, but in the economy as a whole.

The *zaibatsu* were a uniquely Japanese development in economic organisation: vast horizontal conglomerates, presided over by semi-feudal family dynasties, each with a holding company (*honsha*), trading firm and bank at the centre of an extended group of concerns encompassing numerous sectors of industry, commerce and finance. These widely diversified combines were held together by mutual stockholding, personnel ties (such as interlocking directorates), financial bonds and business relationships. The four largest groups — Mitsubishi, Mitsui, Sumitomo and Yasuda — had diverse origins, although their characteristic organisations developed simultaneously during the Meiji period and they were, for the most part, propelled into positions of economic leadership through government patronage. From a solid base in one industry the *zaibatsu* were able to accumulate sufficient capital to expand into further economic sectors, with the ultimate result that by the late 1920s, the heyday of the 'Big Four', most modern industries in Japan were dominated by *zaibatsu* interests.[16]

The centralisation and manipulation of financial power was a key element in the *zaibatsu* model of organisation. The bank was a central, vital component of each *zaibatsu* structure, supplying capital to associated enterprises and employing excess combine funds in productive uses. If the *honsha* could be likened to the nerve centre of a *zaibatsu*, its brain, then the bank would have fulfilled the role of the conglomerate's heart, circulating funds through the organisation and co-ordinating operations by the allocation of credit. The bank also served to 'cement' the combine together, both through the pervasive internal financial arrangements which it managed and, like a secondary *honsha*, through substantial holdings of the securities of associated firms.

In addition, the *zaibatsu* banks were a major source of profits for the combine organisations. As Nakamura Takafusa has shown, the mining, trading and financial concerns were responsible for the majority of profits in the 'Big Four', with subsidiary manufacturing firms contributing a more variable, though consistently smaller share.[17] The banks also assumed the leading role in extending the activities and influence of the *zaibatsu*, as financial leverage was widely used to draw new firms into the conglomerates. Since the *zaibatsu* preferred to expand by absorbing existing productive concerns rather than by creating entirely new ones, the banks' role in leading the growth of the combines, and indeed in ensuring their very survival in the volatile economic environment, was of fundamental importance.[18]

While the *zaibatsu* institutions were the largest and most stable Japanese commercial banks in the first decades of the 20th century, they did not enjoy a clearly oligopolistic position. By 1914, the five largest banks controlled approximately one-fifth of loans and deposits in the 'ordinary' banking system, a proportion which only increased gradually in the years before the rise of militarism.[19] Nevertheless, the four combine banks were clearly the cream of Japanese finance, enjoying special relationships with the most successful industrial firms of the day, nationwide branch networks (at a time when unit banking was still the norm) and a dominant position in securities dealings. The 'Big Four' did not engage in strikingly different practices from other Japanese banks, yet due to their sheer size and prestige were not nearly as vulnerable as the hundreds of smaller 'ordinary' institutions. Thus, the *zaibatsu* banks were able to weather, and indeed profit from, the most severe economic crises of the day, invariably emerging as islands of stability during financial emergencies.

While Japan's private banking structure was, from its foundation, centred on the commercial banks, a range of specialised financial institutions appeared during the Meiji period. Hoping to make provision for the diverse financial services available in the West, the government published regulations for savings banks in 1893 and established the legal foundations for trust banking in 1900. The new types of institutions were not initially a great success, however, as, lacking a clearly defined role in the Japanese system, their activities overlapped with the 'ordinary' banks. Unsound practices and the abuse of privileges were so common that in 1922, after repeated crises, the authorities introduced legislation which delineated stricter standards and more specific functions for both savings and trust banking. *Zaibatsu* interests rapidly came to dominate the reformed banks and by 1930, 60 per cent of savings deposits and 70 per cent of trust assets were held by combine-controlled institutions.[20]

Japan's financial development was not carried forward solely by private initiative, however. In 1931, 40 per cent of all assets in Japanese financial institutions (a share equal to that held by 'ordinary' banks) were distributed among the numerous government financial organs which had proliferated in the Meiji and grown increasingly influential during the subsequent decades.[21] Though functionally and organisationally diverse, these institutions had a common heritage and fundamental orientation. Under the Meiji government, which seldom proved reluctant to assume a direct role in economic development, specialised financial enterprises were founded to supplement existing credit sources, collect personal savings for national uses, take pressure for long-term credit off commercial banks and provide the financial services which private capital could not. Established to further the official economic agenda, and supported by government funding and policy, the public-sector financial institutions developed as potent, aggressive and highly politicised elements in Japanese banking.

The government 'special banks', as they came to be known, were founded at the instigation of Count Matsukata, who believed that such public institutions would efficiently serve the needs of rapid industrialisation and national finance. Under Matsukata's guidance, the government assumed control of the Yokohama Specie Bank, originally a private institution founded in 1880, which concentrated on financing overseas trade. Under official administration, the Bank, granted preferential access to national funds, specialised in foreign exchange business and the encouragement of export industries.[22] In 1897, again at Matsukata's initiative, the Hypothec Bank of Japan was founded on the model of the French *Credit Foncier* to make loans on the collateral of real estate for the promotion of agriculture and light industry. Three years later, the Industrial Bank was chartered (in the form of the *Credit Mobilier*) and charged with granting investment loans to heavy industry. Both these institutions concentrated on long-term lending, raised funds primarily through the issuance of debentures and were firmly controlled by the government.[23] Similarly organised 'special banks' were formed to promote regional development in Hokkaido and the colonies, though these never approached the financial power or stature of the Yokohama Specie, Hypothec and Industrial Banks.

A final government organ of significance was the postal savings system and its adjunct, the Deposits Bureau of the Ministry of Finance. The former was established in 1875, only a decade after postal savings had been pioneered in Britain, to collect funds from individuals through the post office branch network. The system was a great success, as many small savers were apparently more confident in the government than in the private banks, and by 1931, total postal deposits had reached almost ¥3 billion.[24] The collected savings were accumulated in the Deposits Bureau, a fund closely administered by the central authorities, and invested in government bonds and the debentures of 'special banks'.[25] Thus, the Deposits Bureau developed into something of a Finance Ministry 'war chest' which could be used to support officially favoured projects.

In addition to the active direct role in finance which the government maintained through the 'special banks' and Deposits Bureau, the central authorities consistently enjoyed a measure of indirect influence over the activities of private-sector banking. While publicly espousing a *laissez-faire* attitude toward the internal development of the financial system (and indeed rejecting strict legal regulation),[26] the Meiji government was able to affect the evolution of private finance by example, by moral suasion and, probably most significantly, by the judicious use of national financial resources. Such informal, extra-legal methods were particularly important, as the Bank of Japan lacked two key monetary tools — the reserve requirement and open-market operations — under the existing banking arrangements. Much of the government's influence derived, no doubt, from the fundamentally weak position of most Japanese banks and their consequent dependence on official support in times of crisis. Nevertheless, prior to the rise of militarism, the monetary authorities did not have the power or inclination to dictate banking policy to the private sector, seeking rather to advise, encourage and otherwise work obliquely to attain their aims without stifling the dynamism of the financial system.

What was most striking about public-private financial relations during the first 50 years of 'modern' banking in Japan was not so much the extent of official influence as the extent to which a co-operative, constructive atmosphere surrounded dealings between the government and commercial banking. Certainly, the relationship between Japanese bureaucrats and bankers never resembled the cool, detached and sometimes adversarial one which had evolved in the United States. Public and private had been intertwined in Japanese finance since the Meiji period, with extensive historical bonds and an active working dialogue keeping the two sectors closely linked. While the authorities did not always have the same priorities as private bankers, the existence of a basic communality of interests and outlooks kept friction to a minimum and allowed for the development of finance in a manner acceptable to both the bureaucracy and the financial world.

Although the government was able to further many of its economic objectives through the manipulation of the 'special banks', the exertion of its indirect influence or the nurturing of public-private co-operation, the monetary authorities found the stabilisation of finance and the improvement of banking practices problematic.[27] Crises were frequent and even with the government's usual generosity with relief funding, failures were common. Through a process of attrition and consolidation the number of 'ordinary' banks declined from a peak of almost 2,000 at the turn of the century to only 1,300 by 1921.[28] Despite this sobering trend, the majority of institutions were slow to correct their most unsound practices and improve their financial standing, although 'overloan' at least had been controlled by the end of the Meiji period. As government exhortation could not compete with market incentives and pressing obligations, the bureaucracy was unable to greatly accelerate the sluggish pace of change. Ultimately, in 1927, after a decade of economic uncertainty and deteriorating financial standards, the turbulent course of commercial banking culminated in a crisis of unparalleled severity and significance in the development of Japanese finance.

The 1927 crisis was, in the most general sense, a manifestation of the fundamental weaknesses in the structure, functions and official regulation of commercial banking. The existing system of Japanese finance was able to maintain superficial stability during spurts of rapid industrial growth, yet could not adjust readily to the inevitable downswings and periods of economic stagnation. In 1920, following the boom years of World War I, the economy slipped into recession, a serious slump prolonged and exacerbated by the devastating Kanto earthquake of 1923. As the decade progressed and conditions worsened, banking practices deteriorated, unsecured loans and speculative advances increased dangerously, and the need for a major financial readjustment became acute.[29] The collapse finally came in the spring of 1927, when the worst-hit institutions could no longer maintain their façade of stability. In March, a large Tokyo bank failed under the weight of bad debts, causing widespread bank runs and heightening fears of a financial collapse. Some official measures were taken to alleviate private-sector debt, but in April, problems flared again, as the Bank of Taiwan, which had lent freely to a virtually insolvent trading firm, was forced to close its doors. Panic spread and other major banks, including the aristocratic Fifteenth (or 'Peers' Bank'), were driven to suspend business. The Wakatsuki cabinet fell as Japanese finance degenerated into near-chaos. To avert disaster, the Bank of Japan was called to the rescue as usual, injecting nearly ¥2 billion to steady the teetering financial structure and rehabilitate the insolvent Bank of Taiwan.[30]

While the 1927 panic had ended typically, with the government bailing out the commercial banks, the magnitude of this latest emergency forced much critical re-evaluation in both public and private circles. During the crisis the *Manchester Guardian* had described Japanese finance as 'half a century behind the times and unsuited to the modern industrial world',[31] a sentiment which some in Japan regretfully had to agree with. The government, recognising that a revised official role was necessary, thus introduced a new banking law in 1928 to replace the outdated and clearly inadequate 1890 regulations. Under the new code, commercial banks were prohibited from engaging in lines of business not related to banking and minimum capitalisation figures were established for the first time. The government's supervisory powers were greatly increased as the Minister of Finance was given the power to license banks, regulate branching and oversee mergers.[32] Financial reports had to be submitted to the authorities and the government was given the prerogative to conduct bank examinations, a practice which had been notably absent in Japan prior to 1927.[33]

Significantly, the 1928 revision did not set any legal standards for the concentration of loans on a single client, minimum cash reserves, maximum terms for commercial bank advances or the determination of suitable collateral. Although poor bank management had been at the root of the 1927 crisis, the government was unwilling to legislate sound practice, preferring to maintain operational and administrative flexibility within the system.[34] Long-term stability was to be ensured not by raising standards and reforming practices, but instead by reducing the number of 'ordinary' banks, thus concentrating financial resources. Presumably, larger banks in lesser numbers would, both individually and collectively, prove better able to weather Japan's economic fluctuations than the existing rabble of small, undiversified institutions. Thus, while government programmes had promoted bank mergers since 1900, the law of 1928 (through the capitalisation requirements) and subsequent official policy greatly accelerated the concentration process.[35]

The new banking regulations were not intended to force revolutionary change in Japanese banking, but rather to cement superficial stability in the existing financial system. Structural, not operational, reform was the government's solution to instability, thus allowing the 'ordinary' banks to continue their policies of long-term lending, aggressive credit extension, heavy investment in corporate equities and close relations with industry. By accelerating banking concentration the authorities apparently hoped to produce a situation of financial solidity sufficient to allow the traditional patterns of industrial finance to continue indefinitely. The government seemed to recognise that Japanese banking practices, though hardly ideal by English or American standards, had evolved in line with domestic requirements and were suited to conditions of rapid industrial growth. Thus, in the most basic terms, the 1928 reforms amounted to the official rejection of a disorganised, fragmented commercial banking structure but the tacit confirmation of the unique functions, practices and orientations of the Japanese financial system.

The 1927 crisis and the subsequent reforms marked the passing of what might be termed the 'adolescence' of modern commercial banking in Japan. The 'growing pains' of finance were brought to an end, as the government's pragmatic, conservative (and, some might argue, expedient) solutions finally established seemingly lasting stability in banking. The distinct form and nature which Japanese finance had assumed during its half-century of development were preserved and strengthened under the 1928 legal revisions. The banking system thus reached a significant milestone in institutional maturity, with the attainment of firm foundations in finance, a general uniformity of banking practice and an established role for commercial banks in the economy.

As the structure and functions of Japanese banking stabilised after 1927, so too did Japanese attitudes toward financial affairs seem to solidify in the wake of the crisis. Although many appreciated that the banking structure had weaknesses, most Japanese — from financiers to bureaucrats to individual savers — seem never to have questioned the assumption that the ingrained ways were, on the whole, the right ways in Japan. Thus, a concentrated structure, the system of 'indirect' finance and a government active in banking were not seen as aberrations or 'faults', but as essential elements in the established order of the financial world. Japanese views and arrangements may have been unorthodox by British or American standards, yet after all, while Western institutional models had been imported greedily during the Meiji period, Western attitudes toward finance had not been similarly adopted. The Japanese appear to have felt that their banking system was well adapted to local conditions, served the economy admirably and, at least after 1927, offered adequate stability and flexibility. Some critics called for the 'Westernisation' of corporate finance and banking practice but they were, for the most part, voices from the academic wilderness. In the wake of the 1928 reforms, the economic incentives for greater 'Westernisation' were simply not powerful enough to drive significant, lasting changes in banking structure or operations. By international standards, Japan's financial conditions may well have seemed untenable (even after reform), but to the Japanese themselves, with their own ideals, perceptions and expectations, the domestic arrangements 'unsuited to the modern industrial world' were accepted and maintained.[36]

The equilibrium which Japanese banking had attained following the 1927 crisis was soon disrupted, however, by the rise of militarism and the coming of war. In a process which began with the Manchurian Incident of 1931, intensified as aggression in China spread and culminated with 'total war' in the Pacific after 1941, the banking system was 'militarised' under increasingly strict government control. While official intervention in private financial affairs expanded without precedent, the development of banking under militarism otherwise progressed largely along established prewar paths, as characteristic structures, practices and functions were adapted to the demands of war, not entirely transformed by them. Japan's banking system had evolved to provide for rapid industrialisation and was thus suitably prepared to provide the financial support for rapid militarisation as well. Patterns of marshalling and rationing scarce capital resources, concentrating financial power for greater efficiency, operating with a large public-sector contribution to industrial finance and co-ordinating the activities of government and private banking were all established in Japan well before the rise of expansionism, only to be pursued with greater urgency under wartime conditions.

Structural adjustment was rapid during the 15 years of militarism and hostilities. Under strong bureaucratic encouragement to centralise and consolidate financial assets, the process of concentration accelerated in all sectors of private banking. Government policy had long favoured bank mergers, but from 1936, official pressure intensified as the monetary authorities reasoned that a highly concentrated banking structure would prove more efficient and easier to control.[37] The amalgamation programme, pursued under the slogan 'one prefecture, one bank', was highly effective, the number of 'ordinary' banks declining from 1,031 in 1928 to only 61 at the end of the war.[38] Structural developments were much the same in other branches of private-sector banking, with only four thrift institutions and seven specialised trust banks remaining at the time of the surrender.

Under militarism, the *zaibatsu* banks grew spectacularly by aggressively absorbing other institutions and rapidly expanding their operations. The combine banks had profited greatly from the 1927 crisis, attracting much new business by virtue of their prestige and apparent stability, but the war years were a period of unparalleled growth. At least on paper, the 'Big Four' could claim virtually complete financial dominance in commercial banking, controlling 50 per cent of total 'ordinary' bank deposits and almost 70 per cent of advances in 1945.[39] Nevertheless, while the balance-sheet superiority of the *zaibatsu* banks surged forward, their once pervasive influence in finance and industry deteriorated steadily from the early 1930s. As dynamic, new conglomerates developed under military patronage and the 'special banks' expanded their role in industrial finance, the traditional strengths of the combine institutions were undermined and the exclusivity of *zaibatsu* finance was shattered.[40] The continued importance of the 'Big Four' banks cannot be denied, yet their position of financial leadership had clearly been eroded by economic change during the Pacific War.

While the banking structure was forced to adapt to the demands of militarism, the traditional pattern of 'indirect' finance was maintained and strengthened by the wartime bureaucracy. The government recognised that supplying investment funds to industry through the banking system, as was usual, would be more efficient and would allow for stricter central control over credit allocation than any arrangements based on the emission of securities.[41] In the early 1930s some large industrial firms, breaking with tradition, had offered new stock issues directly to the public, hoping to tap new sources of capital and boost their popular image,[42] yet by the middle of the decade, the authorities had choked off the funds necessary to support

13

equity finance on a large scale. The stock exchanges stagnated after 1936 and the bond markets were flooded with government issues, forcing corporate securities out.[43] Under the militarists, the pattern of 'indirect' corporate finance was thus carried virtually to the ultimate extreme. By the last years of the war, with retained earnings dwindling and the 'direct' finance option effectively closed, industrial enterprises were forced into an unprecedented, virtually complete dependence on the banking system for all commercial and investment funding.[44]

In order to supply the vast credit needs of industry during the war, the government readily expanded its direct participation in corporate finance. As private institutions frequently balked at granting the large, potentially risky loans required by munitions and colonial development concerns, the authorities were forced to assume the financing of such essential yet not commercially viable enterprises. The government did not seek to monopolise the funding of industry, but only to respond to the critical requests for capital which the private banks could not or would not fulfil. Toward this end, the activities of the existing 'special banks' were adjusted and expanded while dozens of new, centrally-controlled financial institutions were founded to provide for more-specialised needs. The Industrial Bank took the leading role, particularly in the funding of the pro-militarist 'new' *zaibatsu*, with its advances multiplying an incredible 37 times in a single decade.[45] The Wartime Finance Bank, largest of the newly founded organs, supplemented the Industrial Bank's functions by assuming the riskiest war-related investments.[46] In sum, the government, with its long experience of active participation in industrial funding, showed little hesitation in rapidly and significantly expanding its direct financial role to meet the economic demands of militarisation.[47]

Japan's wartime economy was dominated by the government, which sought to co-ordinate the war effort by extending its influence over private-sector industry and finance. Control over the allocation of credit was recognised as being of prime importance and, as the authorities could not hope to monopolise essential financial functions in 'special' institutions, the bureaucracy worked to broaden and strengthen its leverage over private banks. As the war progressed, the indirect influence in the financial world which the government had maintained since the Meiji period was transformed into direct intervention in the internal activities of the private-sector banking system. The control was not repressive (at least until the last years of the war)[48] yet was pervasive, constricting, and often extended against the wishes of bankers. Nevertheless, the vast increase in government influence was accepted by the private sector as a necessary consequence of war.[49] In the end, this tremendous expansion of official intervention was the most significant development in Japanese banking under militarism, upsetting the balance attained in the prewar years and fundamentally altering the nature of private finance.

Central control was extended legally, financially and administratively through a number of governmental institutions and organisations. The Bank of Japan, as the existing organ most closely involved with private banking operations, assumed the central role in the government's plans to manipulate the financial system. The Bank had never been truly independent of the bureaucracy, but from 1931 was increasingly used as a tool of the militarist administrations to finance national aggression and support the central co-ordination of credit allocation. As Jerome Cohen observed with derision, 'every orthodox tenet of central banking had been violated and the Bank had taken on every conceivable financial chore' in the build-up to 'total war'.[50]

In 1942, the Bank of Japan Law was redrafted to confirm the institution's subservience to the bureaucracy, expand its powers in the financial world and further define its role as an instrument of militarist control. The new law, modelled on the German 1939 Reichsbank Act, decreed that 'the Bank of Japan shall be managed solely for achievement of national aims'[51] and charged it with 'the regulation of the currency, the control and facilitation of credit and finance, and the maintenance and fostering of the credit system, pursuant to the national policy. . . '[52] The Bank's functions were broadened to include participation in industrial as well as commercial finance and provision was made for the Bank to 'undertake such businesses as are necessary for the maintenance and fostering of the credit system'.[53] The supervisory powers of the government were strengthened and codified by the new statutes, as the Minister of Finance was given the authority to set discount rates and currency volume, issue direct orders to the Bank management and dismiss any non-cooperative officers.[54] In sum, the 1942 Law increased the central authorities' control over the Bank of Japan and, in turn, bolstered the Bank's ascendancy over private finance.

As the war progressed, the Bank of Japan became only one locus of governmental control in an ever-increasing web of administrative organisations and legal regulations. After 1936, as Japanese involvement in China intensified, the central authorities sought to systematically tighten their control over the utilisation of funds in the private sector. Thus, in September 1937, the 'Emergency Funds Adjustment Law' was enacted to establish firm central regulation of long-term credit. With the specific aim of choking off funding for non-essential industries, the Law required financial institutions to obtain government approval for large investment loans and subscriptions to corporate securities.[55] In 1940, similar controls were extended over the allocation of short-term capital as well, largely to rein-in the use of credit for speculative purposes. At the same time, strict legal limitations were set on the disbursement of dividends by financial institutions.[56]

While the monetary authorities managed to circumscribe strategically the lending activities of private banking before the Pacific War, full direct control of finance could not be imposed until Japan's links with the international economy were severed in 1941.[57] Thereafter, however, government intervention advanced dramatically, as the meticulous bureaucratic administration of banking emerged as a central feature of the so-called 'New Economic Structure'. In 1942, a 'National Financial Control Association' was established to co-ordinate the activities of private banks with national economic policy. Closely supervised by the authorities, this new body became the prime channel for transmitting official directives to the financial system. The Association was also given specific functions, such as the administration of savings campaigns, war bond absorption programmes and compulsory bank merger schemes.[58] Government control reached its apex in 1944 when, in an act of clear desperation, a system of 'designated banks' was set up to supply the pressing capital needs of munitions producers. Under this plan, 2000 key firms were assigned to 'designated' private institutions (primarily the 'Big Four' banks) which were legally obliged to grant the enterprises unlimited credit, without regard to commercial concerns or standards of safety.[59] Thus, by the last stages of the war, as even the freedom to choose their clients was denied, Japan's banks were finally stripped of all semblance of real autonomy.

In that financial considerations never constrained militarism and war industries never wanted for funds, the government programmes of direct participation and control were a conspicuous success in purely nationalistic terms. Nevertheless, by the end of hostilities the Japanese banking system had been led to the verge of a total, catastrophic breakdown. After 1943, as industry collapsed, inflation flared and the economy slipped increasingly into chaos, the precarious financial foundations of the war effort began to crack. After more than a decade of emergency conditions, the major banks were stretched to their very limits by unending government imperatives to maintain the flow of credit.[60] Under the 'designated banks' scheme, even the largest institutions were hard pressed to preserve their façade of serenity and 'overloan' appeared on a large scale once again. The *zaibatsu* banks, which had taken great pride in their independence during the decades of financial instability, were reluctantly forced to borrow heavily from the Bank of Japan to maintain even minimal liquidity.[61] In the end, the government was only able to prevent a complete collapse by injecting vast quantities of unbacked funds into the economy — a desperate, short-sighted and inadequate remedy for a profound financial malady.

This, then, was the situation which confronted the Occupation in 1945. After 15 years of war finance, the banking system was distorted, imbalanced and ill-prepared for the new demands of peace. Nevertheless, at the core, under the tangle of legal restrictions, accounting contrivances and wartime institutions, the basic financial structures, practices and orientations which had supported Japan's rapid industrialisation and subsequent militarisation remained firmly rooted. The war had certainly brought changes in finance, most notably in the role of the government, but there were considerable fundamental continuities. On the most basic level, Japanese attitudes toward finance were not transformed by the war, as the experience of militarism and defeat did not discredit Japan's banking arrangements or catalyse a critical re-examination of the long-established characteristics of Japanese finance. Bolstered by the weight of traditional outlooks and ingrown conventions, the banking system both remained a critical component in Japan's economic development and retained its unique, 'non-Western' features through the era of militarism and into the years of occupation.

The occupiers, however, were not to look favourably upon the financial apparatus which had so admirably supported Japan's nationalistic aggression. As MacArthur's forces tended to be suspicious of any Japanese institutions which differed structurally or operationally from their American counterparts, the financial sector was to fall under close reformist scrutiny. For although Japan's banking system had proven over time to be economically viable and acceptable to the Japanese themselves, many aspects of the defeated nation's financial arrangements appeared unorthodox by US standards. With the coming of occupation, and the establishment of American values as supreme, the distinctive features of Japanese banking came to be regarded as shortcomings and thus as suitable targets for reform.

2

'Financial Demilitarisation', 1945–8

The American Occupation of Japan approached its task with a victor's confidence, self-righteousness and optimism. The occupiers reached Japan in the autumn of 1945 with lofty, admirable goals and the authority over the defeated nation which appeared to assure ultimate success in any undertaking. Indeed, the potential for fundamental change in Japanese society under American stewardship must have seemed, at the time, to be virtually limitless. Armed with a sense of moral superiority and a very real measure of power, the Occupation fully intended to effect a thorough transformation of its recent enemy.

The Americans considered the existing Japanese economic, political and social structures — described by MacArthur as 'a feudalistic system of totalitarianism which produced results which were almost like reading mythology'[1] — to be irredeemably flawed and antithetical to Western ideals of liberty, justice and peace. The occupiers thus sought to eradicate all vestiges of the discredited past and, as 'architects of the new Japan', refound the nation on the basis of progressive democratic principles. Not surprisingly, the victors chose their own society as the model for their reforms in Japan, seeking (so MacArthur stated) to transplant the 'political, economic, and social concepts which . . . have worked and provided the American people with a spiritual and material strength never before equalled in human history'.[2] With the ultimate aim of establishing a permanently stable and peaceful Japan, the occupiers confidently proposed to break the structures of militarism, educate the people in democratic values and undertake the thorough 'democratisation' of economic and political institutions.

Economic policy inevitably had to assume a significant role in SCAP's ambitious plan for the reorientation of Japan. Nevertheless, American planning was incomplete at the time of Japan's unexpectedly sudden surrender and the occupiers arrived with little idea of the conditions they would face or the actual reform programmes they would have to undertake.[3] The 'U.S. Initial Post-Surrender Policy' of 29 August 1945, Washington's blueprint for the Occupation, assigned SCAP an ambiguous role in the economic sphere. This brief document, hastily prepared during the final two months of hostilities, called for SCAP to pursue Japan's 'economic demilitarisation', the marshalling of reparations and the 'promotion of democratic forces' in labour and industry. SCAP was to hold full authority over the Japanese economy yet, as the 'Post-Surrender Policy' made clear, was not to assume an active role in its stabilisation or reconstruction:

> The plight of Japan is the direct outcome of its own behaviour, and the Allies will not undertake the burden of repairing the damage.
>
> . . . the Japanese authorities on their own responsibility shall be permitted to establish and administer controls over economic activities, including essential national public services, finance, banking, and production and distribution of essential commodities, subject to the approval and review of the Supreme Commander in order to assure their conformity with the objectives of the occupation.[4]

Soon after arriving, however, the Americans recognised that they would be forced to take on greater responsibilities in economic affairs than the pre-surrender planners had intended. The simple programmes which had been sketched out in Washington did not address the complex problems and dire economic conditions which the Occupation faced. The destruction, confusion and dislocation in the economy that accompanied the end of the war clearly necessitated immediate positive action by the occupiers to prevent the nation from slipping into chaos. A stable, productive economy seemed a prerequisite for the broad democratising reforms that the Americans planned, and thus SCAP, from the earliest weeks of its mission, considered economic administration too important to be entrusted entirely to the Japanese.[5]

Despite their admirable aims and broad powers, the economic administrators of SCAP began their work with serious handicaps. Although the broad objectives of demilitarisation and democratisation had been officially established, Washington was unable to supply the occupiers with a well-defined vision of the reformed Japan or a detailed programme for economic change. SCAP personnel were thus forced to hurriedly improvise reform schemes and reconstruction projects, despite an often appalling lack of information on Japanese economic and social conditions. Few Occupation officials had prior experience of Japan or more than a rudimentary grounding in Japanese history and language. Under pressure to take immediate action, but without sufficient background knowledge, SCAP was, not surprisingly, unable to prescribe a ready treatment for Japan's real economic problems and perceived societal ills. Thus, in the first years of occupation, SCAP economic policy was necessarily tentative and often, at least in the eyes of the Japanese, seemingly arbitrary and unsuited to local conditions. Yoshida Shigeru perceptively concluded that,

> The Occupation, with all the power and authority behind its operation, was hampered by its lack of knowledge, and even more so, perhaps, by its generally happy ignorance of the requisite knowledge it lacked.[6]

While the Occupation's authority was nominally complete, its ability to control economic life was significantly affected by the necessity of implementing policy through the Japanese authorities. Throughout the Occupation, the presence of two overlapping bureaucracies, often at odds over policy and locked into an uncomfortable relationship, made the pursuit of economic reconstruction and reform far from smooth. The fact that one of these bureaucracies was rebuilding in the wake of war, while the other was starting anew, certainly contributed to the problematic functioning of the partnership in the early years of occupation.

While the Americans sought to maintain a unified front in their dealings with the Japanese, the internal structure and dynamics of the SCAP administrative machinery made the achievement of true unity in the US camp elusive. MacArthur's civil headquarters in Tokyo was, from its beginnings, fragmented and compartmentalised in a pattern which T.J. Pempel has called 'functional feudalism'.[7] Organised on an essentially military model — but managed with distinctly unmilitary laxity — SCAP was divided into a number of largely autonomous units, each of which was charged with administering a specific aspect of Occupation policy.[8] As one first-hand observer described the balkanisation of the SCAP bureaucracy,

> On the receipt of JCS 1380/15 [an expanded version of the 'Initial Post-Surrender Policy'] the Chief of Staff and his colonels

dismembered its 179 paragraphs and 7,500 words . . . into fragments, and parceled them out paragraph by paragraph to the thirteen staff sections for 'implementation.' The section chiefs and their executive officers divided their assigned paragraphs and sub-paragraphs among their divisions, whose chiefs and executive officers in turn broke their assigned texts even further into assignments for their branches. Sometimes the fragments were as small as a sentence or even a clause. No part of JCS 1380/15 remained unassigned to someone, and almost every branch, division and section had some part of the directive as its 'mission,' even if only a phrase.[9]

Responsibility for the planning and implementation of the American programmes was thus dispersed, the various sectors, divisions and branches of the Occupation bureaucracy laying claim to little 'fief-doms' over the specialised areas of economic, political or social affairs which they had been apportioned. Communications between the various 'domains' were poor and, as the American planners were not always of a single mind, the co-ordination of Occupation policy proved to be time-consuming, frustrating and, in many cases, ultimately unattainable.[10]

Furthermore, the Occupation's work was complicated and con-strained by the serious undermanning of the SCAP economic bureaucracy.[11] Although the American administrative staff totalled several thousand, SCAP was charged with supervising all aspects of the governance of a nation of almost 75 million people. The number of US personnel assigned to Japan might have proven sufficient for the relatively minor, detached role in economic affairs which the pre-surrender planners had anticipated, but the staff levels were clearly inadequate for the more active supervisory role that SCAP found necessary to assume. In the Money and Banking (M&B) Branch of SCAP's Finance Division (ESS-FI), for example, only 20 officials were expected to research, plan and oversee the implementation of Occupation policy on all aspects of banking and insurance. M&B may even have been quite fortunate in its staff allocations compared to other units, as the head of the Economic and Scientific Section (ESS) had cabled Washington at an early stage in the Occupation 'to empha-size the great need for top-flight personnel to be assigned to assist me to cope with problems' in banking and finance.[12]

Some observers of the Occupation have asserted that SCAP's economic bureaucrats were as lacking in quality as they were in quan-tity.[13] Not only did the majority of 'occupationaires' arrive in Japan

21

without prior knowledge of the nation they were to govern, many did not even have formal training or previous experience in the specialised areas of policy that they were asked to administer.[14] The top levels of the SCAP bureaucracy were staffed almost exclusively by military men — members of MacArthur's 'Bataan Bunch' for the most part — whose qualifications for guiding the democratisation and economic reconstruction of Japan were always rather suspect. A classic example was General William Marquat, a career soldier and Chief of the ESS from 1946 to 1952, whose accomplishments in anti-aircraft artillery hardly seemed the perfect credentials for the highest officer in SCAP's economic administration. Among the civilian employees, who eventually came to outnumber uniformed personnel in the Occupation bureaucracy, the time spent in SCAP seemed for many more of an apprenticeship than the apex of a professional life. A number of alumni of the Finance Division went on to successful careers in banking and international trade, but few entered SCAP service with proven attainments in the financial world. Even the harshest critics had to concede that the Occupation employed many able economic administrators, but in general, SCAP had to rely on its staff to be fast learners and competent, even if inexperienced, managers.

In sum, the American occupiers found themselves in the autumn of 1945 soberingly ill-prepared to undertake the supervision and reform of the Japanese economy. Faced with the realities of the situation, the ESS bureaucrats came to realise that Washington's pre-surrender economic planning was simplistic and overly ambitious. SCAP's highest goals had been established in broad terms, but translating the vague ends of 'demilitarisation', 'democratisation' and reconstruction into concrete policies was far from perfunctory. Without a clear overall agenda, the occupiers were forced not only to define their aims and design the programmes to attain them, but also to address somehow the competing (and often conflicting) demands of the multiple American economic objectives. SCAP's efforts to delineate and implement a unified, confident policy were further complicated by the necessity of working through the Japanese authorities, by the existence of 'functional feudalism' and by the handicaps of being undermanned, inexperienced and unfamiliar with Japan. Thus, from the beginning of the US tenure, American economic policy was neither suffused with the pure idealism nor characterised by the consistent singleness of purpose which have traditionally been seen as the hallmarks of the Occupation's reformist mission.

The conditions in the financial sector of Japan's economy were necessarily of great concern to SCAP from the earliest weeks of occupation. Although the banking system did not suffer as acutely from physical damage as Japanese industry, the occupiers discovered it distorted by a decade of war finance and destabilised by defeat. With the surrender, the elaborate 'house of cards' which the Japanese government had devised to finance militarism was poised to come crashing down. While the banks could boast strong statistics on paper — with record deposits and loans — they were all virtually insolvent, holding only worthless government bonds and debts from companies in no position to repay. A nationwide financial crisis, with mass bankruptcies, runs on the banks and the resulting social upheaval, seemed a real threat in the first months, and even years, after the surrender.[15] An emphatic cable to the Joint Chiefs of Staff in October 1945 outlined the emergency in the financial sector:

> Japanese banks are in very bad condition. While ratio of capital to deposits has always been low based on American standards, great increase in deposits and loans during the war has reduced the ratio to approximately one per cent or less. Cash resources are very low. All banks have substantial amount of government bonds which the Bank of Japan will exchange for cash but if a run on banks were to start requiring redemption of bonds to provide currency, great increase in circulation would result and Japanese government would be unable to market new government loans. All banks are carrying as assets loans and securities to concerns which have substantial investments outside Japan. In view of controls over external assets, these concerns may be insolvent and loans uncollectible. Banks also own investment in companies located in non-Japanese area which will have to be written off. If these losses taken probable that banks capital and surplus quickly wiped out. In addition banks have large loans to munitions manufacturers and while many of these are guaranteed by government some of these loans are undoubtedly bad.[16]

As there appears to have been little explicit pre-surrender planning in the US regarding the reconstruction or reform of the Japanese banking system, SCAP was essentially free to establish its own agenda in financial matters.[17] The Occupation's overall goals of demilitarisation and democratisation were naturally the major influence on SCAP planning, but the policymakers in the ESS, and particularly the Finance Division, were also highly sensitive to the immediate practical problems of Japanese banking. Significantly, ESS-FI seems to have

23

realised the importance of a viable, firmly established financial system to the development of a 'democratic, peaceful and stable economy', which was a fundamental American objective in Japan. SCAP recognised that a financial crisis would have jeopardised the success of Occupation reform policy by creating havoc in all levels of business and society.[18] Thus, the Finance Division chose to ignore the punitive, non-interventionist urgings of Washington's early directives[19] and adopt an active, positive role in the stabilisation and reconstruction of the Japanese banking system.

The initial policies pursued by ESS-FI were aimed at what could be broadly termed the 'financial demilitarisation' of Japan. In line with overall policy to eradicate the institutions and influences of militarism, SCAP's economic administrators sought to dismantle the financial machinery of the war years and redirect the banking system toward peacetime functions. Given the status of the banks and the legacy of ten years of war finance, attempting to pacify and simultaneously rehabilitate the banks was clearly a formidable challenge. The financial situation demanded immediate attention from the authorities yet required cautious and precise official handling. Hasty, ill-conceived attempts to break the economic relationships and structures of war finance could have proven disastrous, exacerbating rather than easing the banking dilemma. A total overhaul of the system was needed, but the ESS and the Japanese government were forced to move cautiously lest their policies for demilitarisation push the fragile financial network to collapse. Thus, SCAP had to orchestrate a delicate surgical operation on Japanese finance, removing the pervasive, tenacious remnants of the war economy without crippling the patient in the process.

The demilitarisation of finance was complicated, moreover, by the runaway inflation that was unleashed by the collapse of wartime controls. The inflation, which rose even into triple digits in the first years of occupation, affected all levels of society and endangered the precarious stability of the economy. Washington was alarmed by the situation and advised SCAP in November 1945 that 'Serious inflation will substantially retard the accomplishment of the ultimate objectives of the occupation.'[20] The ESS's highest priority in reconstruction policy, therefore, was to bring the inflationary spiral under control. Demilitarisation of banking clearly took a subordinate position, but the two programmes were inextricably linked, as anti-inflationary policy was necessarily exercised through financial channels. As a result, SCAP policy sometimes appeared a compromise between pressures for price stabilisation and financial readjustment that addressed neither issue in an optimal manner.

Under these circumstances, SCAP encountered difficulty in adopting and maintaining a consistent policy for financial demilitarisation. Although ESS-FI's basic intentions seemed clear from early in the Occupation,[21] the programme only took shape over time and did not follow the dictates of a specific 'master plan'. There was no Japanese equivalent of the 1946 Colm-Dodge-Goldsmith Report, the exhaustive American blueprint for financial reorganisation in Occupied Germany.[22] Seen in retrospect, however, the SCAP policies do show a kind of order and logical progression which would appear to indicate that the Finance Division bureaucrats were guided by some constant, if not formally elaborated, principles and objectives. The programme which ultimately evolved seems to have been essentially two-fold. The first step was to stabilise the banking system, rationalise government finances and temper the inflation as quickly and thoroughly as possible, using direct controls and Occupation fiats whenever necessary. Once the threat of a major economic crisis had been minimised, SCAP then planned to break the financial bonds of the war years by what one document termed a 'catharsis' — cancelling the government's indemnities and allowing banking and industry to reorganise on a peacetime basis.[23] This scheme was compatible with the occupiers' overall agenda, as the demilitarisation and readjustment of Japanese finance could be accomplished without the generation of new inflationary pressures or the creation of extreme dislocations in the economy and society.

The Japanese government fully concurred with the Americans' basic goals of stabilising the banking structure, averting a financial crisis and re-establishing a peacetime economy. The Japanese could not show the same enthusiasm for all of the economic policies which SCAP put forward, however, and were in strong disagreement with key elements of the American programme. Perhaps most significantly, the Japanese government did not share the Occupation's eagerness to control inflation and exhibited what the ESS considered reckless abandon in its fiscal and monetary policies. The Japanese position was forcefully advocated by Ishibashi Tanzan, editor of the *Oriental Economist* and Minister of Finance from 1946–7, who believed that stagnation, not inflation, was the greatest economic threat to Japan following the defeat. Ishibashi, preaching a variety of fundamentalist Keynesianism, held that the nation suffered from the under-utilisation of productive resources and could only be pulled from its postwar doldrums by great infusions of government spending. Without sufficient pump-priming by the government, the Japanese maintained, financial institutions would be bankrupted, working capital would evaporate and, as a result, production would grind to a halt.[24] The Japanese stance was no doubt determined by political considerations in addition to economic theorising, as successive governments certainly appreciated that expansionary programmes would inevitably prove more electorally popular (and less socially disruptive) than strict policies of fiscal conservatism.

Therefore, in the first months following the surrender, the Japanese government continued and even accelerated the payment of its obligations from the war years. The disbursements included demobilisation allowances, settlements of outstanding wartime contracts and indemnities for cancelled munitions orders and bombing damage. The pay-out was huge: in the space of only three months, the government pumped ¥26 billion into the economy, a figure estimated to be about one-third of Japan's total military spending in the war years. Legitimate sources of government revenue were virtually exhausted by 1945 and the bulk of the government's payments was financed through the Bank of Japan's creation of new, unbacked money. Thus the success of the Japanese policy in forestalling the threatened stagnation was spectacular, as the price level increased almost six-fold in the last five months of 1945.[25]

The spending spree came to an end in November, when SCAP finally recognised that the government's finances were the source of the rapid inflation. The Japanese authorities were instructed to suspend the payment of all military pensions immediately. Further, in a directive headed 'Elimination of War Profits and Reorganization of National Finances', the Americans ordered that no government war obligations be paid except into special blocked bank accounts supervised by the ESS. Tight controls were imposed on all areas of Japanese government finance, as the authorities were forbidden to borrow funds, extend loans or establish new subsidies or tax exemptions without the Occupation's approval.[26]

These SCAP directives were the first in a long line designed to restrain the Japanese inflation through the imposition of direct controls on government activity and the workings of the private-sector economy. Many ESS bureaucrats were former employees of Roosevelt's 'New Deal' administration, with a philosophical commitment to central planning and the judicious use of direct controls to promote social equity and economic efficiency.[27] As the Japanese authorities did not share the Americans' preoccupation with price stability or their esteem for 'democratic' central planning, however, success was impossible under the 'New Dealers' ' strategy unless all aspects of fiscal and monetary policy could come under close SCAP surveillance. Without sufficient personnel or knowledge of the Japanese economy to achieve this level of supervision, SCAP was repeatedly frustrated in its anti-inflationary policy by the Japanese government's ability to undermine, side-step or conveniently ignore the Occupation's controls.

Thus, after SCAP had clamped down on the post-surrender spending binge, the Japanese shifted to monetary policy as the spearhead of their expansionary effort. When the government was forced to suspend disbursements, its creditors in the private sector turned to the commercial banks for the operating funds which they required. The banks, though suffering from a decrease in deposits with the acceleration of inflation, were willing to increase their advances to commerce and industry. The financial institutions were able to expand credit because of easy money policies adopted by the central bank. The *Oriental Economist*, expressing the feelings of Ishibashi and the Japanese government, stated in early 1946 that:

the continued adherence by the Bank of Japan to its lenient credit policy . . . is the primary reason why our economy after the war's termination, although face to face with a crucial situation, has managed to sail clear of the rock until today.[28]

As a result of the government's expansionary policies, the economy remained flooded with money and inflation continued unabated into 1946. In February, however, SCAP implemented a bold initiative to absorb the excess purchasing power in the hands of the public and, in so doing, to neutralise the inflationary effects of Ishibashi's relaxed fiscal and credit programmes. The Occupation's ambitious plan, resembling the Belgian monetary reforms of 1944, aimed to sharply reduce the volume of money in the economy through a currency conversion, and gain long-term control of the free money supply by the strict regulation of bank deposits. As one prominent periodical reported, though perhaps with some overstatement, the programme was 'not only the most noteworthy economic event since Japan's surrender but also involved change with few parallels in scale in Japan's economic history'.[29]

Under the Emergency Financial Measures Ordinance of 26 February 1946, all personal and corporate bank accounts were frozen and cash withdrawals were limited to small monthly amounts adjusted in proportion to family or enterprise size. Immediately following the initial blocking of deposits, a partial currency conversion, which allowed each individual to exchange only ¥100 of old yen for new notes, was enforced. Under these measures, in theory, cash funds held in excess of ¥100 per person were forced into the banking system prior to the conversion, as afterwards the old yen notes ceased to be legal tender. Since all deposits were blocked, the currency pressed out of the economy, as well as that already in the banks, then came under governmental control.

The 1946 monetary reforms were an important step in the stabilisation and readjustment of Japanese banking.[30] The blocking of accounts solidified the financial position of the banks, which had been suffering from consistent decreases in deposits, by assuring them of a stable deposit base. Furthermore, the partial currency conversion caused almost ¥46 billion in new deposits to enter the financial system — a windfall utilised by the major banks to reduce their indebtedness to the Bank of Japan.[31]

On the macroeconomic level, the immediate effects of the emergency financial measures proved dramatic and entirely satisfactory to the planners of the ESS. By the end of March 1946, the note issue had declined to only a quarter of its pre-conversion peak, Bank of Japan advances to the financial sector had been drastically reduced and, most importantly, inflation seemed to have at last been moderated. The Tokyo Wholesale Price Index, which had increased 166 per cent in the first quarter of 1946, rose only 36 per cent in the second and 21 per cent in the third. The respite was short-lived, however, as the Japanese (with the tacit approval of their government) soon discovered ways around SCAP's controls over deposits. Despite repeated American efforts to tighten the restrictions on withdrawals, the note issue and money supply regained their previous highs by August, assuring a fresh burst of inflation.

Nevertheless, the relative stability of mid-1946 afforded the Finance Division the opportunity to begin the second stage of its 'financial demilitarisation' — the cancellation of government indemnities and the thorough reorganisation of the banks. SCAP encountered firm opposition, however, from the Japanese government, which seemed committed to making good on its wartime indemnities. The Japanese economic bureaucrats were motivated in part by a sense of honour, as they felt the government had to meet its financial obligations to show its good faith and preserve public confidence. Probably more importantly, the government, and particularly Ishibashi, believed that the payment of the indemnities would make a significant contribution to Japan's economic rehabilitation. As with the massive disbursements following the war, the 'inflationists' in the Japanese bureaucracy maintained that full settlement of the indemnities would pump much-needed funds into the industrial sector, promote production and buoy up the financial institutions.[32]

The Americans were resolved to stop the payment of the government's wartime obligations, however. SCAP felt that the full payment of the indemnities would appear to reward those who had economically supported militarism, and thus undermine American efforts to nurture a peace-loving mentality in the Japanese people. In addition, the Occupation's economic analysts knew that full restitution could not be undertaken without crippling government finances and causing an unprecedented burst of inflation. The sums involved were huge: at the end of the war, the private sector claimed ￥70 billion in indemnities, a figure which exceeded the estimated ￥65 billion total war damage to national wealth and was three times the central government revenues for 1945.[33] Clearly, any significant settlement of the indemnities would have forced the Japanese government to resort to the printing presses and was thus totally unacceptable to the stability-conscious economists in SCAP.[34]

The debate over the cancellation of the indemnities raged from the beginning of the Occupation to the autumn of 1946. The Japanese considered the indemnities issue to be of critical economic importance, yet after months of discussion and deliberation, the government was reluctantly forced to bow to SCAP's authority and resolution. Ishibashi remained adamantly opposed until the end, taking a harsh anti-Occupation stance for which he would later be purged, and as Minister of Finance refused flatly to cancel the obligations in full. As a compromise, SCAP agreed that the payments could be nominally made by the Japanese, thus preserving the façade of good faith, but that a 100 per cent tax would immediately be levied upon them. As a further concession, the Americans granted certain private-sector creditors small exemptions from the tax, creating loopholes which allowed for the eventual disbursement of the unexpectedly substantial sum of ￥18 billion.[35] In the end, however, the bulk of the outstanding war indemnities was wiped away at a stroke, as the Occupation planners had wished.

Naturally, such a vast write-off was certain to have tremendous economic consequences and immediate, co-ordinated action by the authorities was necessary to prevent a total financial collapse. The effective cancellation of the war indemnity payments forced much of industry into insolvency, which in turn rendered virtually all financial institutions bankrupt. The effects of SCAP's programme on the banks should not be underestimated, as more than two-thirds of the loan balance of Japanese banks represented financing of munitions companies or wartime insurance advances.[36] Therefore, prior to the announcement and implementation of the indemnities scheme, SCAP and the Japanese authorities had to devise a comprehensive financial reorganisation plan for the government, industry and banking.

The blocking of deposits under the emergency financial measures had been the first step toward a full reorganisation of the banks, and in August 1946 revised regulations were issued in advance of the enactment of the indemnities tax. All restricted bank accounts were separated into two categories: Class A blocked deposits, which remained subject to the provisions of the February financial measures and were considered current accounts; and Class B blocked deposits, which were completely frozen, with no withdrawals permitted. Households were allowed ¥15,000–32,000 each (depending on family size) and companies a flat ¥15,000 each in Class A deposits, the remainder going into Class B blocked accounts.[37] At the end of September 1946, following the segregation of accounts, 43.7 per cent of total bank deposits were under the designation Class A; 13.7 per cent were Class B; 18 per cent were in free accounts (deposits made after the currency conversion); and the remaining 26 per cent were in the special blocked deposits for indemnity payments.[38] The goal of this restructuring was to allow continuation of business in the 'new account' — Class A and free deposits — while the liquidation of wartime liabilities was carried out in the 'old account' — Class B and special blocked deposits.[39]

Thus, with provision made for the financial functioning of the economy during the reorganisation of the banks and industry, SCAP moved on to the financial stage of its plan. On 18 October 1946, the Japanese government enacted the Law for the Reorganization and Reconstruction of Financial Institutions, the most significant piece of legislation affecting banking since the surrender.[40] In essence, this law, drawn up primarily by the Finance Division of SCAP, was the blueprint for the final 'demilitarisation' of the Japanese banks' tangled accounts. An Occupation report concisely stated the planners' intentions:

> The major objective of this law was to promote the development of a stable economy and the maintenance of adequate living standards through: (1) the realistic revaluation of the assets of financial institutions in the light of existing economic conditions; (2) the preparation of reorganization plans by the financial institutions for the approval of the government; and (3) the distribution of losses

in accordance with a system of priorities established by the law.[41]

Under the reorganisation statutes, the banks first had to determine their losses on loans to firms bankrupted by the war indemnities tax and on investments made in colonial and wartime enterprises.[42] Once the total of these 'special losses' from the war years had been established, the law allowed the banks to liquidate them in a carefully prescribed procedure for writing off liabilities, the objective being to bring 'new account' liabilities into line with sound assets. The 'special losses' were borne first by retained profits and reserves, then by the shareholders (up to 90 per cent of capital) and finally by the creditors, first from Class B blocked deposits and then from the 'new account' if necessary. Under this system, shareholders and larger creditors (that is, those holding Class B deposits) sustained losses before the smaller creditors.[43]

In the end, the total 'special losses' were found to exceed ¥25 billion, with the share of the Industrial Bank alone ¥7.5 billion, and the *zaibatsu* banks' combined total ¥9 billion. In the liquidation, eight banks were able to reorganise without writing off any deposits, 56 were forced to write off 90 per cent of their capital and some Class B blocked accounts, and four found that they could not meet their wartime losses.[44] The authorities ultimately agreed to indemnify the few institutions rendered totally insolvent to the extent that deposits in the 'new account' would not be affected by the reorganisation.[45]

Such a major operation was, in itself, a procedural and accounting nightmare, but the process was further complicated by the authorities' insistence on overseeing the programme at each step. Consequently, progress was very slow, though with the provision for a 'new account', the bulk of the economy was not seriously affected by the banks' internal re-orderings. The reorganisations were completed for all practical purposes by mid-1948, when the 'new' and remaining 'old' accounts were finally merged and unfrozen, and the banks were allowed to recapitalise.[46] Japan's financial institutions were thus restored to a reasonably stable peacetime footing, with ordered internal finances and relatively strong assets. Certainly by historical standards the Japanese commercial banks had attained a respectable level of financial, structural and procedural stability. Although the demilitarisation process had been long and complicated, the progress made in the strengthening and readjustment of the banks during the three years after the surrender was, in retrospect, quite impressive.

While the ESS-FI plan for 'financial demilitarisation' stressed the rehabilitation of private-sector banking, the Americans did not exhibit

31

similar enthusiasm for the revival of Japan's government-controlled financial institutions. Indeed, one of the Occupation's first dictates in Japan was an order to close the various institutions which had served as the financial arm of Japanese militarism and overseas aggression. Included under the directive (SCAPIN 74) were the mammoth financial organisations which had been founded to fuel Japan's war effort and maintain its controls in the colonies: the Wartime Finance Bank, the United Funds Bank, and all 'other financial institutions whose paramount purpose has been the financing of war production or the mobilization . . . of financial resources in colonial or Japanese occupied territory'.[47] In all, approximately 260 wartime institutions were targeted by ESS-FI for liquidation, with total assets of ¥450 billion.[48] As the figures suggest, the scale of the operation was tremendous and even two years after the surrender, the liquidation of wartime institutions was described in an ESS report as one of the most pressing problems in the banking field.[49] Although direct SCAP involvement had ceased by 1948, the process of dismantling structures and settling accounts continued under Japanese stewardship until 1952, when all the institutions' assets were finally liquidated.

Although Japan's four oldest 'special' banks had contributed generously to the war effort, they were spared dissolution under SCAPIN 74, presumably because they had not been chartered specifically for wartime purposes. Nevertheless, SCAP soon realised its omission and pressed the Japanese to close these institutions as well, viewing them as active collaborators in the military conspiracy and potent tools for manipulative government intervention in the private economy.[50] Once again, however, the Japanese position was at odds with the American, for while the authorities recognised the folly of preserving specialised wartime institutions in a peaceful economy, they could not easily tolerate the elimination of the historically important 'special' banks.

Like the indemnities question, the fate of the four banks — the Yokohama Specie, Hypothec, Industrial and Hokkaido Colonial — became the subject of prolonged and intense controversy between the occupiers and the Japanese bureaucracy. A compromise favourable to the latter was eventually reached, as the Japanese managed (albeit with some difficulty) to convince the ESS administrators that the 'special' banks performed essential functions in the financial system and deserved rehabilitation. Thus, while the four designated institutions were legally abolished, each was allowed to continue operations in a somewhat altered state, though all were stripped of their official privileges and formal ties to the government. The Hypothec and

Hokkaido Colonial Banks were re-chartered in 1948 as 'ordinary' institutions and concentrated on commercial financing, while the Yokohama Specie, which emerged from reorganisation as the Bank of Tokyo, was allowed to retain its specialisation in international activities.[51]

The Industrial Bank constituted a special case, however, for SCAP recognised its significance as a central co-ordinator of the war effort and was therefore suspicious of Japanese motives in promoting its reconstruction.[52] In order to save this crucial institution, the Japanese resorted to what one author termed an 'adroit waiting game' — sheltering the Industrial Bank in a dormant state while SCAP opposition was 'neutralised' by official entreaties for leniency.[53] The occupiers were eventually worn down and the Bank, after several years as a bond-issuing organ, was resurrected in 1950 as the first of a new breed of long-term credit institutions. Legal ties to the government were broken, but as extensive personnel and financial bonds were maintained (and indeed since the Bank had been salvaged only through official intervention), the Industrial Bank remained an economically influential, 'kept' institution of the bureaucracy. As Kent Calder concluded, the failure to dissolve the Industrial Bank must rank as one of the 'most paradoxical omissions' of SCAP's work to demilitarise the Japanese economy.[54]

A final noteworthy aspect of the Occupation's financial demilitarisation plan, and one which seems comparably 'paradoxical' in retrospect, was the effort to break the government's wartime controls over the loan policies of commercial banks. The 'New Dealers', it seems, approved of central controls only when used toward progressive, 'democratic' ends, or perhaps more precisely, only when necessary for the achievement of US policy in Japan. Thus, SCAP sought to dismantle the militarists' restrictive systems of 'designated' financial institutions, compulsory loans and bureaucratic control over private credit. SCAPIN 863 of 5 April 1946, which abolished the elaborate structure tying banks to munitions firms, stated:

> The development of a vigorous industrial and commercial structure . . . requires that the government shall not interfere with the basic economic right of a borrower to secure credit from any willing lender and of a lender to extend credit to any sound borrower. Development of a free and independent banking system adjusted to the varying needs of local communities and adhering to sound loan and investment policies is regarded as a vital step in the renewal of peacetime production and the democratization of the Japanese economy.[55]

SCAP soon found, however, that under the Bank of Japan's easy money policies and without strict government regulation, the banks became too casual in their extension of credit:

> Private banks, unable to resist quick profits, have been extending credit indiscriminately for all purposes. Similarly, large zaibatsu banks are under constant pressure to overextend credit to zaibatsu-affiliated companies.[56]

Thus, as a counter-inflationary measure, and in the hope of directing funds into more productive uses, SCAP found it necessary (and in no way hypocritical) to support renewed, active credit-control policies.

The Ministry of Finance, which had only relinquished its wartime controls under US pressure, also strongly believed that re-imposed restrictions on credit allocation were necessary, although for somewhat different reasons than the Americans. While control of inflation was hardly a major concern, the bureaucracy was eager to re-establish its authority to direct private-sector loans to certain industries and enterprises. Under the so-called 'priority production scheme', the fulcrum of Ishibashi's economic plan, the Japanese government sought to focus scarce commodities — in this case bank credit — on key industries which would form the basis for a broader recovery. Thus on 1 March 1947, with the occupiers' tacit approval, the Ministry issued detailed new regulations to financial institutions regarding the supply of capital to private concerns. Under these rules, industries were divided into three groups, with those considered most important under 'priority production' — steel, coal, fertiliser — given preference in the supply of funds for working capital and equipment investment. Industries considered peripheral to overall recovery, or non-essential, were allowed only very limited amounts of commercial bank loans.[57]

These government guidelines, though less restrictive than wartime controls and not focused on munitions production, were essentially very similar to the militarists' regulations, particularly those of the 'Emergency Funds Adjustment Law' of 1937. While the Occupation authorities recognised a need for renewed allocative controls, SCAP was critical of the extent and usage of the Japanese regulations of 1947. A report from the Money and Banking Branch of ESS-FI expressed concern that the strict controls might be regarded as 'a return to the "Designated Loan System" which is considered unacceptable in principle'.[58] Perhaps even more galling to SCAP was the fact that the financial arrangements for 'priority production' actively promoted neither the reduction of inflation nor the growth of 'democratic forces' in Japan. Nevertheless, the guidelines did seem to produce a more efficient distribution of credit and, with strong Finance Ministry support, were intensively utilised until 1949 and thereafter used selectively until their repeal in 1963.[59] While the postwar regulations did not constitute a full revival of the wartime controls, their significance in the late 1940s and their lingering presence suggest that SCAP's efforts at demilitarising the government's relations with private finance were not wholly successful.

Overall, however, the Occupation's programme of financial demilitarisation managed to re-establish stable conditions and free the Japanese banking system from the most crippling legacies of the wartime economy. By 1948, the banks had been restored to a solid financial basis and prepared for a constructive role in Japan's postwar revival. The government, meanwhile, was released from the huge burden of wartime debt and industry was transferred to solid new financial foundations. Perhaps most remarkably, SCAP's work in banking and finance did not engender fresh waves of inflation, threaten social stability or cause serious disruptions in the industrial recovery. Just as financial arrangements had never proven a constraint to Japanese militarism, so the ESS-FI seems to have ensured that the 'pacification' of banking did not prove a barrier to postwar reconstruction. Considering the extent of the task and the dismal conditions, handicaps and complications which the economic administrators of SCAP faced, the various accomplishments of the American demilitarisation plan constituted a notable achievement.

Nevertheless, the Occupation's 'financial demilitarisation' was incomplete from a reformist standpoint and its work, though important, was essentially superficial. SCAP did not (and perhaps under the circumstances could not) turn back the clock to 1931, reversing entirely the changes in banking structure, practice and function which derived from the needs of militarism and war. Thus, despite American claims of complete success in demilitarisation, the 'special' banks were resuscitated, government financial controls were re-established and the *status quo* in commercial banking was not upset. The Finance Division worked from a narrow definition of 'demilitarisation', limiting its work to what was obvious, what could be accomplished with relative ease and what was compatible with the officially favoured programmes of inflation control and institutional democratisation. The liquidation of wartime banks and the financial reorganisation were essentially complicated exercises in accounting which, in effect, merely enabled the wartime financial system to function under peaceful conditions. In other words, the occupiers accomplished adjustment, not transformation. American demilitarisation supplied a bridge, rather than forced a break, in the continuing evolution of Japanese banking.

A more ambitious, rapid and thorough demilitarisation of Japanese finance was apparently not even contemplated by the economic administrators of SCAP. The essential reorientation or transformation of banking did not, after all, figure prominently in US plans for postwar Japan. In the first three years of the American tenure, the Occupation's top priority was clearly the democratisation of key political and social institutions, with economic policy relegated to a supportive role. Therefore, intending to create conditions conducive to 'revolutionary' democratic change, the ESS pursued normalisation of the economy and the maintenance of stability as its prime economic concerns. Rehabilitation of the banking system was, of course, crucial to these efforts and was installed as the fundamental goal of the occupiers' initial financial programmes. The Americans did seek the demilitarisation of Japanese banking, but only so far as it contributed to the reconstruction of finance and the eventual attainment of US objectives in Japan.

Thus, from the earliest months of the Occupation, the Finance Division of the ESS approached banking policy with a cautious, determined and pragmatic outlook uncommon in SCAP, seeking effective, immediate solutions to the many problems of post-surrender finance. Not surprisingly, ESS-FI discovered that the most expedient and surest manner of addressing the Japanese financial dilemma was by working within the established banking structure. As the financial network was so fragile following the war, the Finance Division considered the strengthening of the existing banking system the least disruptive, safest option for creating stable 'normalcy'. Certainly, this relatively unambitious, conservative approach was a complete success in the sense that a ruinous financial crisis was avoided and the difficulties of banking never hindered US democratisation projects. Although Yoshida Shigeru criticised the occupiers for often 'multiplying the confusion which . . . already existed' in Japan,[60] such was apparently not the case with the Finance Division's first programmes of banking rehabilitation.

The American overseers of Japanese finance were certainly aware that reconstruction and stabilisation were not the sole economic objectives of the Occupation, as indeed initial US directives had enjoined SCAP to encourage democratic developments in the economy, as well as in government and society. Nevertheless, financial democratisation was clearly of secondary importance to the bureaucrats of ESS-FI in the first years following the surrender.

While the Finance Division recognised the potential need for structural and legal reform of Japanese banking, it maintained that the stabilisation and peacetime readjustment of the financial world must precede any major reform programmes.[61] The potential benefits of a financial overhaul were, it seems, not thought to justify the possible risks — seen in terms of social and political instability — of its implementation. At any rate, without sufficient pre-surrender planning, an adequate knowledge of domestic conditions or the co-operation of the Japanese authorities, SCAP was not initially in the position to offer any specific, well-reasoned proposals for the transformation of the wartime banking system. ESS-FI seems to have adopted policies in line with the Occupation's greater reformist goals when practicable — as in the preference given to small depositors in the financial reorganisation — yet democratising reform was never adopted at the great expense of the Division's more pressing economic objectives.

By limiting the scope of 'financial demilitarisation', postponing reform and bolstering the existing arrangements in Japanese banking, the Finance Division may have cost SCAP the opportunity to direct significant structural or legal reform of the Japanese financial system. The Americans' greatest economic democratisation efforts were pressed forward in the two years immediately following the surrender, when conditions in Japan were the most fluid, SCAP's directive abilities were the strongest and change seems to have been the easiest. While the land reform and antitrust programmes were surging ahead, however, a narrowly business-like, pragmatic attitude prevailed among the group most responsible for banking policy. Detached from the crusading SCAP reformism, the bureaucrats of ESS-FI worked to strengthen the entrenched structure and functioning of the Japanese financial system. Such an approach may have been the most effective for the stabilisation and readjustment of the economy, yet in later years, the essentially conservative nature of the Finance Division's early programmes proved to make the Americans' attempts at banking reform all the more difficult.

3

The Banks and the Antitrust Programme, 1945–8

Perhaps inevitably, the pragmatism of the Finance Division came into conflict with the reformist thought that pervaded SCAP in the early years of the Occupation. While ESS–FI was labouring to rehabilitate the financial system, other elements in the SCAP bureaucracy were working, with equal determination, to transform the fundamental character of Japanese society. The democracy which these Americans sought to foster (or, some would argue, impose) encompassed all aspects of Japanese life — from government and the economy to law, education and even culture. As the financial sector occupied such a pivotal position in the economy, it eventually came under the scrutiny of SCAP's reformers; and as Japanese banking appeared so closely linked with the interests of the *zaibatsu*, it seemed a natural target for the Americans' programme of economic democratisation.

The concept of economic democracy, which the Occupation was attempting to export to Japan, had deep roots in the American political ethos. An economy of free enterprise and open competition has traditionally been seen in the United States as conducive to the functioning of the democratic political system and consonant with the American ideal of personal freedom. Great concentrations of economic power vested in corporations or individuals have often over the last century been viewed by the public as threats to the 'American way' of liberty, individualism and economic opportunity. Franklin Roosevelt, who directed an active antitrust policy under the 'New Deal', captured the spirit of American feelings:

This concentration of wealth and power . . . has been a menace to the social system as well as to the economic system we call American democracy . . . The struggle against private monopoly is a struggle for, and not against, American business. It is a struggle to preserve individual enterprise and economic freedom[1]

This philosophy — with its mistrust of 'big business' and faith in competition — was eventually passed down to the occupiers of Japan. SCAP was also the inheritor of what Ted Cohen described as the 'New Deal conviction that political reforms are inadequate and only fundamental economic changes could be effective'.[2] Establishing the American model of economic democracy was thus assumed to be an essential step in the process of transforming Japan into a peaceful, stable and thoroughly democratic nation. In General MacArthur's view,

> . . . if business in Japan were allowed to continue with its concentration of economic power, it would lead to concentration of power in government, and from there the transition to socialism of one form or another would be natural, easy of accomplishment, and inevitable.[3]

The *zaibatsu* had no place in the American vision of a reformed Japan. To the occupiers, the combines were semi-feudal institutions whose vast economic power and political influence had stifled democracy and freedom in prewar Japan. A substantial share of the responsibility for the rise of Japanese militarism was ascribed to the *zaibatsu* system, which, the Americans maintained, provided an economic setting favourable to military aggression and materially supported Japanese expansionism. The economic structure was assumed to have shaped — or rather, to have warped — social development, with one crucial Occupation report concluding,

> Something has been seriously wrong with the social system of Japan . . . Doubtless no single condition is responsible for these peculiarities. The excessive concentration of economic power in Japan is, however, one of the more important factors.[4]

Professor Corwin Edwards, a key advisor on US antitrust policy for Japan, summed up criticism of the *zaibatsu*, stating:

> Japan's industry has been under the control of a few great combines, supported and strengthened by the Japanese government. The concentration of control has encouraged the persistence of semi-feudal relations between employer and employee, held down wages, and blocked the development of labor unions. It has . . .

39

retarded the rise of a Japanese middle class. In the absence of such groups there has been no economic basis for independence in politics nor much development of the conflicting interests and democratic and humanitarian sentiments which elsewhere serve as counter-weights to military designs. Moreover, the low wages and concentrated profits of the Zaibatsu system have limited the domestic market and intensified the importance of exports, and thus have given incentive to Japanese imperialism . . . They necessarily became instruments of their government in international politics. They necessarily served its purpose in order to be loyal not only to Japan but to their own profits.[5]

Policy regarding the combines was one of the few economic issues relating to Japan that was extensively considered in Washington prior to the surrender. Although relatively little was known about the functioning of the Japanese economy, specialists in the State Department had begun analysing the significance of the *zaibatsu* as early as 1943. The American planners, primarily economists recruited from academic positions and the 'New Deal' bureaucracy, had progressive economic views and were predisposed to be suspicious of 'big business'. The existence of huge corporate concentrations of power in both Germany and Japan seemed to confirm their belief that institutions such as the *zaibatsu* and the *konzerns* were antithetical to democracy and supportive of militarism. The economists' conclusion was that the inordinate industrial, financial and political influence of the Japanese combines, like that of their German counterparts, would have to be shattered under American administration.[6]

In the 'Initial Post-Surrender Policy', the State Department's position on *zaibatsu* reform was officially endorsed and transmitted to the Occupation forces:

Encouragement shall be given and favor shown to the development of organizations in labor, industry, and agriculture, organized on a democratic basis . . . To this end it shall be the policy of the Supreme Commander . . . to favor a program for the dissolution of the large industrial and banking combinations which have exercised control of a great part of Japan's trade and industry.[7]

As in the case of economic demilitarisation, SCAP was presented with a broad statement of objectives rather than a concrete set of policies to implement. The onus of policy-making was thus placed squarely on the Occupation bureaucracy, yet once again SCAP proved unprepared to tackle its responsibilities immediately. Without adequate knowledge of the *zaibatsu*, and lacking the personnel to marshal the necessary information rapidly, SCAP's initial actions on *zaibatsu* dissolution were nebulous and unassertive.

In contrast, the four great *zaibatsu* reacted quickly and firmly to the American policy of economic democratisation.[8] Though the *zaibatsu* houses naturally opposed the dissolution of their vast economic organisations, the leaders of the combines realised that some change was inevitable. Rather than waiting for SCAP to determine a dissolution programme, which the Japanese feared would be sweeping and punitive, the *zaibatsu* decided to take the initiative and propose a voluntary scheme for structural reform. By designing their own reorganisation plan, the *zaibatsu* believed that they could win the goodwill of SCAP's reformers and limit the real effects of the Occupation's antitrust policy.[9]

In October 1945, Yasuda became the first of the *zaibatsu* to present a blueprint for voluntary dissolution. The Yasuda plan, which was subsequently endorsed by the other major combines, comprised four programmes for breaking the internal bonds of the 'Big Four' *zaibatsu* superstructures: first, the *honsha*, the combines' top holding companies, were to transfer their massive security portfolios to a newly-created Holding Company Liquidation Commission (HCLC) for eventual public sale; second, the *honsha* were to cease the exercise of control over their former subsidiary enterprises; third, the existing directors and auditors of the holding companies were to resign their offices; and, finally, the members of the four old *zaibatsu* families were to relinquish any positions of influence which they held in the business world.[10]

The Yasuda plan was designed to appeal to SCAP's reformers without seriously upsetting the operations of the *zaibatsu*. While the plan was presented as being a comprehensive solution to the problem of economic concentration, it only addressed a single element in the vast *zaibatsu* networks. The Yasuda scheme did prescribe dissolution for the *honsha* and the severance of some key vertical linkages in the combine structures, but it did not aim to disturb the extensive economic influence of the prime *zaibatsu* subsidiaries in finance, industry or trade. In essence, the *zaibatsu* strategy was to sacrifice the holding companies in order to preserve the greater bulk of affiliated operating concerns intact. Thomas Bisson, in his pioneering work on the antitrust programme, concluded that the Yasuda plan had 'dextrously shifted dissolution action from the combines to the holding companies'.[11]

41

Despite its omissions, the Yasuda plan was welcomed enthusi-astically by the Americans, gained rapid Occupation approval and was transmitted to the Japanese government for immediate implementation as SCAPIN 244 of 6 November 1945. Although Colonel Raymond Kramer, Marquat's predecessor as Chief of the ESS, praised the Yasuda leadership for its 'courageous determination' in accepting 'great sacrifices' voluntarily,[12] the American reformers were quick to realise that the dissolution of the *honsha* would not alone ensure the democratisation of the Japanese economy. To the combines' great disappointment, the occupiers made it clear in SCAPIN 244 that further programmes of reorganisation and deconcentration would be necessary. While the document presented no specific plans, it affirmed SCAP's commitment to extensive structural and legislative reforms which would 'provide equal opportunity to firms and individuals to compete in industry, commerce, finance and agriculture on a democratic basis'.[13]

SCAP's confident statements on antitrust policy seemed rather hollow, however, for although the occupiers had learned a great deal about the *zaibatsu* by the end of 1945, they had as yet devised no overall blueprint for the democratisation of the combines. The Japanese realised that American reformism had not been tempered by the solicitous stance they had initially affected and further 'voluntary sacrifices' were not forthcoming. Therefore, hoping to avert the stagnation of antitrust policy as SCAP groped for suitable reforms and the Japanese became increasingly un-cooperative, the Washington bureaucracy dispatched a delegation to Japan charged with formulating a comprehensive dissolution plan for the Occupation.

The State-War Mission on Japanese Combines, which spent three months in Japan in early 1946, was composed of technical experts from Washington regulatory agencies, with a noted authority on anti-trust policy, Professor Corwin Edwards of Northwestern University, as its leader. The Edwards Mission, as it was commonly known, produced a short analytical paper on the structure of the combines and a concise list of policy recommendations designed to 'effectively destroy the power of the zaibatsu'.[14] Though modest in volume, the Mission's report was a crucial document, forming the basis of American antitrust policy in Japan for the following two years. The Edwards findings gave direction to the previously unfocused, rather disordered *zaibatsu* dissolution programme by articulating clear goals and establishing a comprehensive agenda for achieving them.

Significantly, Edwards and his colleagues sought to extend and enlarge the scope of the American antitrust initiative. The Mission appraised the Yasuda scheme as a far from satisfactory first step, and set about devising a plan to 'remedy as rapidly as possible [its] omissions and weaknesses'.[15] The dismantling of the holding companies was considered only the beginning, as Edwards prescribed similar procedures for operating companies which, 'standing alone, still enjoy a monopolistic position or are so large as to retain much of the combines' power'.[16] In addition, the Mission's report greatly broadened the definition of what constituted a *zaibatsu*. Whereas SCAP had previously focused its attention almost exclusively on the four oldest and largest family-controlled combines, Edwards extended the title '*zaibatsu*' to encompass 'any private enterprise . . . which, by reason of relative size in any line or the cumulative power of its position in many lines, restricts competition'.[17] In short, the Edwards Mission recommended that Occupation antitrust policy should be expanded from a limited administrative reorganisation of the 'Big Four' *zaibatsu* to a comprehensive attack on all centres of economic concentration in Japan.

After establishing this broader scope for American antitrust efforts, the report set out a three-faceted plan for the democratisation of the Japanese economy. First, the Mission called for the breaking of all ownership, personnel, contractual and financial ties within the combines, a process which had been started with the Yasuda plan, but which Edwards sought to expand to intersubsidiary linkages. Second, thorough deconcentration of the economy was to be achieved by breaking outsized operating companies into small units which would not 'constitute a material or potential threat to competitive enterprise'.[18] Finally, a democratic, free economy was to be ensured in the long term by the enactment of suitably strict antitrust legislation and the foundation of responsible and powerful regulatory bodies.

Although the Edwards recommendations addressed all sectors of the Japanese economy, financial institutions came under particularly intense scrutiny. Prior to the Edwards Mission, the antitrust reformers in SCAP appear to have given relatively little thought to the democratisation of Japanese banking, although this had been clearly established as an American objective in the 'Initial Post-Surrender Policy' and reaffirmed in the JCS policy directive to MacArthur of November 1945.[19] In the first months of occupation, SCAP did request statistical information from the largest commercial banks, but apparently with no intention of initiating a reform programme. As one Finance Division memorandum stated, 'No analysis of the Sumitomo or Mitsubishi banks is planned by the Cartel Division, but only a determination of their place in the zaibatsu.'[20] While the

Yasuda plan, which had originated in the most financially-involved of the combines, was carefully designed not to affect the banks, the Occupation reiterated the official commitment to the structural reform of finance in SCAPIN 244. At this early stage, however, the occupiers had as yet given little attention to financial democratisation and SCAPIN 244 attempted to pass the burden of planning to the Japanese government, ordering it to prepare a programme for the reorganisation of Japan's banking giants. As the Japanese authorities were hardly eager to collaborate with the Americans on antitrust policy, this aspect of the directive was conveniently ignored.

With the coming of the Edwards Mission, however, the banking system was subjected to close reformist scrutiny and the first specific proposals for the democratisation of Japanese finance were produced. The Mission's report offered a vigorous condemnation of virtually all aspects of the existing banking structure, while singling out the 'Big Four' *zaibatsu* banks as prime targets for antitrust action. The Mission, marshalling substantial statistical data, asserted that the combines' banks dominated Japanese finance and used their control over funds to uphold the economy's oligopolistic structure and prevent the emergence of 'democratic' competition. Edwards identified the advantages derived by the *zaibatsu* from their ascendancy in the financial world as

(1) preferential access to bank credit, particularly when money is tight or when the subsidiary which wishes to borrow is too weak to be a good credit risk; (2) ability to squeeze independent concerns by withdrawing credit in times of stringency; and (3) ability to exercise over many of their competitors the surveillance which a banker may impose upon a borrower.[21]

In addition, Edwards noted that the control of banking had been critical to the emergence, development and maintenance of the *zaibatsu* form of organisation. Recognising that the 'Big Four' financial institutions were centres for the co-ordination of combine activities and bulwarks of the *zaibatsu* structures, the Mission concluded that

. . . the zaibatsu banks occupy a key position in zaibatsu enterprise, that they are securely fixed in their respective combines by a multitude of ties and that they constitute a source of great strength to their related enterprises.[22]

The Edwards report proposed breaking the financial power of the *zaibatsu* with an array of programmes in line with its three-faceted plan for economic democratisation. To sever the 'alliances' between banks and other enterprises, the Mission advised SCAP to place strict limitations on the amount a bank could loan or invest in an individual company, on the percentage of a firm's outstanding shares which a bank could hold and on the outside positions which bank officers could assume. Financial deconcentration was also recommended, though on this point, the Mission's suggested policy line was somewhat vague:

> The number of sources of credit should be increased substantially. For this purpose, former owners of independent financial institutions which have been merged with zaibatsu concerns should be permitted to re-establish their old enterprises by forced divestitures. If this expedient proves insufficient, other devices should be used also — possibly a requirement that banks over a given size must split themselves into two or more independent units within a stated period.[23]

Finally, the Mission advised legislative reforms that would eliminate discrimination in favour of the *zaibatsu* banks, reduce governmental interference in the financial system and set a new, competitive standard for commercial banking.

The report of the State-War Mission was published in March 1946 and although SCAP initially found the proposals somewhat ambitious and 'academic',[24] the occupiers readily embraced the Edwards plan as a suitable blueprint for reform. Due to practical constraints such as the undermanning of the ESS, however, SCAP was forced to proceed with the implementation of the Mission's recommendations in a gradual, piecemeal fashion. Thus, during 1946, the American reformers concentrated on efforts to eradicate the administrative, ownership and personnel bonds which knit together the *zaibatsu*. As Edwards had recommended, SCAP expanded the coverage of the Yasuda plan to include not only the great *zaibatsu honsha* but a range of other holding companies as well. In September and December 1946, SCAP designated a total of 83 firms — including the co-ordinating concerns of the 'new' *zaibatsu* and large combine-controlled industrial enterprises — as holding companies which would be subjected to the provisions of the Yasuda plan.

The Yasuda scheme, however, provided only for the elimination of vertical linkages and so, in accordance with the Edwards proposals, SCAP had to take separate action to break the extensive networks of horizontal ties which existed between *zaibatsu* operating firms. In

December of 1945, the Occupation designated all companies with capitalisation of ¥5 million and above (approximately 1,200 firms in all) as 'restricted concerns'. These enterprises were instructed to furnish regular financial information to SCAP and were subject to certain restrictions, such as prohibitions on merging with other companies or rapidly liquidating corporate assets. In November 1946, following recommendations of the Edwards Mission, this 'schedule of restricted concerns' became the basis for SCAP's programme to shatter the *zaibatsu*'s inter-subsidiary networks. Under Ordinance 567 of 25 November 1946, the restricted concerns were ordered to divest of all their stock holdings, their affiliates were required to dispose of recently acquired securities and their officers were barred from holding concurrent positions in multiple firms.[25]

Thus, through securities divestment, management reforms and various minor measures, the expanded list of holding companies and the 'restricted concerns' were to be deprived of their 'anti-competitive' linkages and control functions. The actions were not comprehensive, however, as the financial sector was curiously spared from the brunt of the occupiers' 1946 *zaibatsu* initiatives. Although the banks' extensive stockholdings and personnel connections with *zaibatsu* enterprises made them seemingly obvious targets, no financial institutions were designated as holding companies. Furthermore, while the *zaibatsu* banks and insurance companies had been included in the 'schedule of restricted concerns', they were subject to more generous treatment under Ordinance 567 than other firms. In particular, the restricted financial institutions were required to dispose only of the stock of companies 'in their own chain of capital', that is, within their associated *zaibatsu*.

Authors writing on the American antitrust policy have been at pains to explain why the banks were not more severely treated under the SCAP programmes of 1946. Considering the importance placed on reform of the Japanese financial system by the Edwards report, this omission is surprising and, to some commentators, very disappointing. There is, however, no clear, simple explanation for what Eleanor Hadley terms the 'preferential treatment' which SCAP gave the *zaibatsu* banks.[26] Documentary material on SCAP antitrust programmes prior to 1947 is elusive, and what is easily available tends not to address the banking issue specifically. Hence any efforts to explain the curious loophole given to banking in the 1946 reforms must be based largely on conjecture.

One influence on SCAP programmes which must always be considered is the role of the Japanese government. In antitrust policy, as in so many other areas, the Japanese authorities did not share the aims or approve of the methods of their American counterparts, and hence worked against the imposition of reform in what ways they could. Japanese opposition to the dissolution programme was based on the impression that the policy was essentially punitive and would seriously hamper the country's industrial recovery. As the concept of 'economic democracy' was unknown and the reputed benefits of 'free competition' unproven to the Japanese, the bureaucracy was quite understandably sceptical and fearful of US reform efforts. The Finance Ministry was particularly critical of SCAP policy and was dedicated to preventing the radical reform of Japanese banking. The Ministry was not opposed to all change, however, and from the outset of the Occupation, some officials recognised that the separation of the banks from the *zaibatsu* interests could be a positive step. One Ministry of Finance internal report stated that

> . . . even if the zaibatsu were to be dissolved, it is natural and necessary that, in view of their public and national nature, zaibatsu financial institutions be maintained, that they be made purely financial institutions and deprived of their 'zaibatsu color' completely.[27]

The Japanese bureaucracy was clearly against the dissolution of large financial institutions but, sensing possible benefits from loosened *zaibatsu* bonds, apparently decided not to confront the occupiers over plans for breaking the banks' networks of intra-combine control. There is no evidence to suggest that the Ministry of Finance took a strong stand on this matter, nor any reason to believe that the American reformers would have been deterred by any such approach at that time. Thus, the relatively lax treatment of the 'Big Four' banks in the 1946 programmes seems unlikely to have stemmed from extreme Japanese government opposition.

Most probably, the anomalous treatment of the banks in 1946 can be traced back to the influence of the Finance Division of SCAP. From the beginning of the Occupation, ESS–FI had assumed *de facto* control of the planning and implementation of all SCAP policy affecting the financial system. As noted earlier, the Antitrust and Cartels Division (ESS–A/C), which directed the Occupation's *zaibatsu* programme, showed little reformist interest in the banks during the first years of the American tenure. As ESS–A/C apparently declined any role in financial policy, ESS–FI could lay claim to 'eminent domain' over questions pertaining to banking within the 'feudal' bureaucracy of

SCAP. Consequently, in 1946 the Finance Division not only held a virtual monopoly in the American camp on information concerning the banking system and on experience working with Japanese financiers, but also had a 'proprietary interest' in Occupation banking policy. Naturally then, when increased reformist attention was focused on the *zaibatsu* banks, the 'trust busters' would have looked to ESS–FI for counsel and, indeed, the Finance Division would have jealously demanded to be consulted on any planning for banking reform.

The Finance Division took a characteristically pragmatic position on antitrust action, holding that banking should be considered separately from the other constituent elements of the *zaibatsu* and treated uniquely according to the circumstances.[28] While ESS–FI seems to have considered the breaking of the combines' internal ties an admirable objective, it maintained that the fragile banking system should be handled cautiously and with a full appreciation of its peculiarities and special problems. The Finance Division believed that the reforms of banking directed by Ordinance 567, though less stringent than the conditions imposed on other concerns, were sufficient to attain SCAP's immediate antitrust goals. Writers such as Hadley and Bisson have lamented SCAP's lenient treatment of the banks in 1946, but ESS–FI clearly believed that the reformers' objectives in finance had been accomplished under the limited measures of Ordinance 567:

> The alliances between financial institutions and commercial concerns have been broken due mainly to two policies which have been put into effect. The first is the taking over and sale of stock held by Zaibatsu interests . . . The second policy prohibits the holding of office in more than one organization so that a director of a bank cannot be the director of any other enterprise . . .[29]

Any harsher line, such as designation as holding companies, might have impaired the banks' ability to fulfil their role in the economy by constricting their necessary functions or upsetting public confidence. A heavy-handed approach would have been unacceptable to the bureaucrats of ESS–FI who, as discussed in Chapter 2, seemed to be amenable to reform only when it did not interfere with essential rehabilitation.

Although the 'trust busters' began to show increased interest in banking policy during 1946, the Finance Division's exclusive 'feudal' domain was not really challenged by the reformers until the following year. In April of 1947, however, in a personnel change which was to have a profound effect on the course of the American *zaibatsu* dissolution programme, Edward C. Welsh assumed the post of Chief of SCAP's Antitrust and Cartels Division. Prior to Welsh's appointment, the leadership of ESS–A/C had been held in turn by two army officers who exhibited little enthusiasm for reform and whose combined tenure amounted to less than a year. Welsh was to be the Division's 'permanent' chief and he approached his position with an aggressiveness and tenacity which seemed to be lacking in his short-lived predecessors. As a former economics professor, advisor to the Temporary National Economic Committee and staffer at the Office of Price Administration, Welsh's 'New Deal' credentials were impeccable and his faith in the social and economic benefits of anti-trust reform unquestionable. Under his vigorous leadership, the Antitrust Division was to pursue change with greater intensity, some would say fervour, than ever before. By 1947, ESS–A/C had gained some confidence in its ability to reform and, with the appointment of Welsh, a dedicated, sincere and able chief.[30]

The bureaucratic changes in SCAP coincided with equally important developments in Washington. While the Occupation was dealing with the holding companies and 'restricted concerns', the State Department was revising the Edwards recommendations for approval as official US policy. The final policy document, officially designated SWNCC 302 (though more commonly known as FEC 230, a later redesignation), was in most respects a mere restatement of the Mission's proposals. In the financial area, however, the State Department planners prescribed even stricter measures than Edwards had, perhaps intending to rectify SCAP's relatively lenient treatment of the banks in 1946. SWNCC 302 called for more stringent restrictions on bank lending and investment and more extensive legislative reform than the Edwards group had proposed. Most significantly, the final policy statement took a strong line on the deconcentration of banking, an area which Edwards had left rather vague. SWNCC 302 stated plainly that forced deconcentration would be necessary:

> Banks over a size to be specified by SCAP should be required to split themselves into two or more independent units within a stated period, as should other banks deemed by SCAP to enjoy a monopolistic position in the field which they serve. The permissible size should be set at a level sufficiently low to force a significant number of such actions and thus greatly increase the number of independent sources of credit . . .[31]

Welsh fully embraced the American policy set down in SWNCC 302 and immediately began work to realise the document's provisions. The breaking of internal *zaibatsu* ties was quite well advanced by the time Welsh took over, as was the preparation of the comprehensive Antimonopoly Law (enacted April 1947). Thus, the new Chief of ESS-A/C focused his division's energies on the third facet of the plan originally outlined by Edwards and confirmed by SWNCC 302: the deconcentration of centres of excessive economic power.

As Welsh was aware of the intense indigenous opposition to further antitrust action, he concluded that the desired deconcentration would have to be forced upon the Japanese through the imposition of a rigorous, SCAP-designed programme of legislation.[32] Toward this end, Welsh prepared 'Standards for Economic Reorganization' (for commercial and industrial concerns) and a companion 'Standards for Excessive Concentrations in Banking Fields' which set down specific criteria for determining which firms SCAP would seek to 'democratise' by partition. Welsh showed no reluctance in including banks in his plan and the standards for financial institutions were very strict:

> Any private banking enterprise . . . will be considered an excessive concentration if it meets any of the following criteria . . .
> 1. Has lending capacity sufficient that if it were withdrawn from the credit market an uncontrolled commercial loan rate would rise substantially or hardship would be imposed upon legitimate users of credit.
> 2. Has sufficient influence and power in its field of operations that it could take action which would make it difficult for another entrepreneur to enter the same field of activity with reasonable opportunity to compete successfully.
> 3. Acquired other organizations, operating units or concerns . . . and enjoyed special privileges as a result of war mobilization policy, since 1937.
> 4. Has sufficient cumulative influence and power over the flow of commercial credit . . . to affect significantly the relative growth of individual companies as compared with other companies in the same field of endeavor.[33]

The criteria demanded the evaluation of Japanese banking against standards of competition maintained nowhere else in the world, including the United States.[34] Provisions 1, 2 and 4 set impossibly high standards, suggesting that their author would have been satisfied with nothing less than perfect competition in the financial sector. Provision 3 was very tidily designed to ensure that the *zaibatsu* banks and other important financial institutions would be targets for structural reform. Indeed, the strict application of these standards would have led to most, if not all, of Japan's commercial banks being considered 'excessive concentrations'.

Welsh's document, while in line with the official policy of SWNCC 302, offered as the basis for the ESS-A/C financial deconcentration plan a set of expectations which was clearly unrealistic. As Welsh intended that each institution found to be a centre of excessive power under these criteria would be broken into smaller units, the full application of his 'Standards' would logically have led to the atomisation of the Japanese banking system. This may have been Welsh's goal, as he seems to have looked to an idealised form of American unit banking as his model for the reformed Japanese financial structure:

> Banks should be organized so that primary direction of the bank management is to serve the local public on a non-discriminatory basis in relationship to the credit needs of that area . . . It is not in the interest of banking management efficiency nor in the interest of deconcentration to have bank operations of any one bank extend generally throughout a large geographic area.[35]

Welsh completed the 'Standards' in May 1947 and immediately set to work on the legislation which would ensure their application to Japan's economic structure. The Japanese were unified in their opposition to Welsh's plan, but the Antitrust Division draft of a deconcentration law was nonetheless presented to the Diet in October, and subsequently passed, under SCAP coercion, on 9 December 1947.[36] The 'Elimination of Excessive Concentrations of Economic Power Law' (commonly called Law 207) authorised the HCLC to establish uniform criteria and designate as excessive concentrations the appropriate firms in all economic sectors, irrespective of *zaibatsu* affiliation. Each designated concern was required to submit plans for its own structural reorganisation, preferably a division into a number of new, independent enterprises. The proposals were to be scrutinised by the HCLC and, if approved as constituting sufficient 'democratisation', were to be carried out by the designated concerns.[37]

While Law 207 applied equally to all sectors of the Japanese economy, SCAP indicated that banking was to be handled under a special procedure. Possibly due to Finance Division recommendations,

MacArthur decided that the application of Law 207 to the banks would have to be delayed for practical reasons. In a 26 January 1948 cable to the Department of the Army, the Supreme Commander reported:

> Plan is to require HCLC to designate industrial companies first, distributive and service companies second, insurance companies third and banks under a special procedure . . . Banks probably to be affected by deconcentration now are reorganizing pursuant to provisions of the Financial Institutions Reconstruction and Reorganization Law and major changes necessary to eliminate excessive concentration characteristics are being effected insofar as practicable. Objective is to conduct reorganization of banks to maximum degree possible before public announcement is made in order to prevent loss of public confidence in banking structure or in any banking institution.[38]

Furthermore, while Law 207 required the HCLC to publish its criteria for designation and reorganisation, MacArthur stated that 'standards for financial institutions will not be made public initially'.[39] Thus, when in February 1948 the Commission released its standards, showing just minor rewording from Welsh's earlier drafts, only criteria for the designation of industrial and commercial enterprises were given.

The delays in the extension of Law 207 to the banks apparently had the support of the Antitrust Division, which was in the process of formulating a comprehensive plan for the structural reorganisation of Japanese finance. ESS-A/C seems to have concluded that a broad, systematic reform of the banking structure was preferable to a series of independent, un-coordinated reorganisations undertaken by individual designated banks. As early as December 1946, ESS-A/C had requested advice on such a programme from the Research Division of the ESS,[40] and by the beginning of 1948, following the clarification of deconcentration goals in Law 207 and Welsh's 'Standards', a preliminary plan was produced.

The Research Division's report was highly critical of the Japanese banking structure, going much further than even Edwards' condemnation. The paper held that,

> The facts of the situation are: Excessive concentrations in Japan developed in and through banks . . . Retention of present national network of banks would leave intact the major tool for other zaibatsu.[41]

The plan did not echo Welsh's unrealistically strict definition of what constituted an excessive concentration in banking, but targeted only the very largest banks with nationwide branch networks, particularly the four *zaibatsu* institutions and the Sanwa Bank. The higher powers in SCAP appear to have supported this more practical approach, as MacArthur's cable of January 1948 stated that, of the banks, 'six will probably come under the classification of excessive concentrations'.[42]

The Research Division report, like Welsh's 'Standards', was preoccupied with the geographical aspects of Japanese banking. The paper suggested that national branch banking, as it existed in Japan, retarded the development of a competitive, free-enterprise system, while a structure of predominantly unit banking, as existed in the United States, was conducive to 'economic democracy'. The writers were clearly mistrustful of a centralised financial system — exhibiting a typically American suspicion of the shadowy world of 'high finance' — and maintained that the concentration of financial power in Tokyo and Osaka discriminated against provincial customers and enabled the state to exercise undue influence over banking.[43]

The report's policy recommendations called for a vast structural change in the Japanese banking sector. Perhaps due to a lack of information, the Research Division's proposals were not fully refined, and offered a concept rather than a concrete, practicable programme. The report suggested that Japan be administratively divided into between three and eight banking districts. Each Japanese bank would be allowed to maintain branches and engage in business within only one of these zones, as in the US, where a bank's operations are legally limited to a strictly-defined geographic area. Therefore, each of Japan's large institutions with nationwide branch networks would be forced to split into several independent regional banks based within the newly established boundaries. The concentrated power and influence of the *zaibatsu* banks would thus be divided and dispersed, allowing, the report maintained, for the flourishing of competition and 'economic democracy' in the Japanese financial system.[44]

ESS-A/C espoused the Research Division's plan and released it within SCAP on 9 February 1948. Welsh had made sure that ESS-FI officials were not consulted during the preliminary planning process (aware, no doubt, of their conservative tendencies) and the Division was shocked when suddenly presented with a document outlining substantial reforms of the banking system.[45] On 19 February, after analysing the proposal, the Chief of ESS-FI, Walter LeCount, submitted to General Marquat an extended critique of the Antitrust

Division's programme. In his memorandum, LeCount found fault with virtually every aspect of the ESS-A/C report, asserting that its writers did not understand the nature of the Japanese financial system and had thus devised a totally unsuitable and impractical course of action.

The memorandum began by offering evidence to refute what LeCount termed the 'major premises' of the reform plan. The Finance Division held that there were no 'excessive' concentrations of banking power in Japan, noting that as of 30 September 1947, the nine largest banks controlled only 38 per cent of total deposits, with Yasuda Bank, the single largest, holding only 7.1 per cent.[46] The critique maintained that financial power was dispersed among the city, prefectural and special banks, the savings institutions and the nearly 25,000 credit co-operatives. ESS-FI did not see Japanese banking as oligopolistic: 'The big banks are actually highly competitive for both loans and deposits, since they operate side by side in the majority of the cities and prefectures.'[47] Further, the memorandum discounted the view that a system of nationwide branch banking is antithetical to free enterprise and healthy competition, offering the example of Canada.

The Finance Division thus held that forced deconcentration of the banks was unnecessary, as no 'excessive' concentrations existed and the Japanese system of branch banking was not, *per se*, incompatible with economic democracy. LeCount argued further that the provisions of SCAP's 1946 programme for breaking internal *zaibatsu* ties and 1947 antitrust legislation had surely accomplished enough to prevent the re-emergence of the combines:

> The banks' policies are established by the board of directors acting on the advice of shareholders. The shares formerly held by the Zaibatsu are now controlled by the HCLC, which will sell them to the general public. This dispersion will destroy any vestige of control by the Zaibatsu interests.
>
> It is to be assumed that the new antitrust laws will prevent the formation or perpetuation of industrial combines, so that it is not necessary to perform surgery upon the banks which financed them.[48]

The memorandum concluded with a consideration of what seems to have been the Finance Division's prime concern — the possible economic repercussions of the ESS-A/C plan:

> [The Antitrust Division report] proposes that branch banking by private banks be limited to specific areas. While such an idea may

sound good to some in theory, its impracticality makes it financially most unsound. The recommended program is of such a dangerous nature that if followed it is considered that complete financial collapse would in all probability ensue. At the present time the Japanese Government and private enterprises are faced with a very serious credit and economic condition. This condition would be further aggravated by the freezing of credits, further losses created by the forced liquidation of loans and a tremendous loss to depositors resulting from forced liquidations, which could only result in a complete undermining of the confidence of the people in the banking structure. If production of industry is to be increased and foreign trade expanded, it is most necessary to have sound banks able to finance their activities. The paralyzing effects on the banks which would follow a limitation on specific areas of branch banking would be adversely felt by the entire economy of Japan.[49]

In sum, after two years of working to rehabilitate the Japanese banks and stabilise the financial structure, the Finance Division was hardly prepared to accept a plan which, in its opinion, would unnecessarily cripple the banking system.

Tristan Beplat, Chief of the Money and Banking Branch of ESS-FI during 1946 and 1947, has commented that the Finance Division viewed the reform proposal as an attempt to copy policy in occupied Germany.[50] The similarities were obvious, as in Germany the Allies imposed regulations which allowed commercial banks to operate branches in only one *land*. The three largest German banks, which, like the *zaibatsu* institutions, had nationwide branch networks and pervasive financial influence, were broken down into 30 'successor' banks. The consequences of the German deconcentration seem, in retrospect, to confirm the Finance Division's gloomy predictions of the economic repercussions of the Antitrust plan in Japan. As one financial historian summarised the adverse side-effects of the German reform,

. . . it increased the demand for bank cash and other liquid assets, since smaller banks felt the need for a larger margin of safety; senior bank management now had to be allocated to each of the successor institutions, which meant that it had to be spread around much more thinly . . .; it was felt that working efficiency had been impaired and that the banks had thereby lost goodwill; it was expected that the smaller banks would also have to charge higher

55

rates of interest and this would drive up borrowing costs.[51]

A contemporary critique of the German reform by Hans Adler could just as easily have been applied to the ESS-A/C proposals for Japanese finance:

> [The banking programme] has not found the approval and coopera-
> tion of the German authorities. Officials in Military Government
> expected this, but hoped that they could enforce it over a lengthy
> period so that the Germans would, in time, recognize it as workable
> and accept it as beneficial. However, . . . the reorganization is
> contrary to the trend of events in all other industrialized countries,
> including the U.S. Not only has the independence of local institu-
> tions been severely reduced and the control of central institutions
> strengthened everywhere, but the interference of the state in the
> financial affairs of the nation has become more direct and exten-
> sive. The reorganization of banking in Germany seems now like
> an unnecessary and futile attempt, the success of which assumes
> conditions which have not existed for a long time and which are
> not likely to return in the foreseeable future. It is doubtful whether
> the well-meant attempt has a chance of survival.[52]

Indeed, following the Occupation, the West German authorities permitted the recentralisation of the banking structure, a process of readjustment which required almost a decade to complete.[53] In the end, the reforms may not have shattered Germany's economy, but they did cause severe dislocations which retarded recovery and, with the post-Occupation reconcentration, did not even manage to implant permanently what the 'trust busters' considered a 'democratic' banking structure.

Welsh's Antitrust Division and LeCount's Finance Division therefore came down squarely on opposite sides of the banking deconcentration issue. The reformers insisted that the financial struc-ture would have to be reorganised or the success of the entire economic democratisation programme would be put in jeopardy. The bureaucrats of ESS-FI argued with equal emotion that the deconcentration of banking was a superfluous addition to the antitrust effort and that any significant structural reforms would cripple the reconstruction of the financial system. Neither side exhibited much flexibility in its stand, prompting LeCount to write Marquat in March 1948 that,

> It is considered that the continuation of discussions between A/C

and Finance Divisions on the method of reorganizing banks gives little promise of being compromised due to fundamental differences.[54]

Although it seems that a bureaucratic deadlock had developed, the Divisions continued discussions on the banking deconcentration issue. In the second week of April, a working group with representatives from both sides was formed to explore the Antitrust Division's plan in more detail. Since the release of its study in February, ESS-A/C had been clarifying and refining its programme and presented to the group a tentative plan for the reorganisation of the Yasuda Bank. The Antitrust representatives proposed that this institution be dissolved and replaced by three new banks — one based in Tokyo with branches limited to the Kanto area and north; a second headquartered in Osaka with offices in central Japan; and the third bank located in Fukuoka with operations in Southern Honshu and Kyushu. The Finance Division agreed that such a plan was technically possible, though SCAP would have to impose it upon the Japanese. The ESS-FI representatives were not convinced, however, that such a scheme was either necessary or advisable. LeCount reported:

> From the facts and discussions presented, Finance Division feels strongly that the plans or ideas for the breaking up of the branch banks advanced by Antitrust are not practical or feasible, especially under present economic conditions in Japan but will be highly effective if the objective is the disintegration of the banks.[55]

The working group thus broke down in failure, with no easy resolution to the internal dispute in sight. The debate was much complicated by the fact that neither division had clear jurisdiction within the SCAP organisation over policy relating to the banks. The Finance Division claimed that it held sole responsibility for Occupation banking policy, having administered financial programmes since the surrender. The Antitrust Division, on the other hand, had shown little interest in banking until 1947, yet Welsh believed that it was responsible for the formulation and implementation of democratisation programmes in all sectors of the economy, including finance. The actual responsibilities and functions of the various constituent parts of the ESS had never been satisfactorily defined and there was no established procedure for settling disputes which resulted from unclear or overlapping jurisdictions. When, as in this case, two feuding divisions found themselves diametrically opposed on policy, indecision and paralysis usually afflicted the planning process until a mutually acceptable compromise was reached, or the higher authorities stepped in with a final pronouncement.[56]

In the debate over banking reorganisation, both divisions realised the impossibility of reaching a compromise and focused instead on presenting their cases to the higher ranks of the ESS.[57] Thus, throughout the spring of 1948 General Marquat was bombarded by Welsh and LeCount with memoranda, reports and proposals on the bank deconcentration issue. With the bureaucratic deadlock, Antitrust and Finance looked to the Chief of the ESS for a decision:

> Finance Division considers that further discussions of the various possibilities and theories, such as have been advanced by Antitrust representatives, can lead to no practical results and again strongly urge that a policy decision be made in the immediate future so that all possible actions can be taken to forestall any further demoralizing effects upon the banks resulting from a continuation of the uncertainties involved.[58]

Marquat was reluctant to take a stand, however, and despite the volume of material on banking reform which crossed his desk, he was slow to intervene in the debate. Through the first months of 1948, even after both divisions had reported that attempts at compromise had broken down, the Occupation leadership did not provide a resolution, but rather stepped back to let the internal dispute continue.

The unresponsiveness of the higher echelons of SCAP appears to have stemmed from indecision and caution. For while the Antitrust and Finance Divisions were looking to MacArthur's headquarters for guidance, the SCAP leaders were similarly turning to their superiors in Washington for direction. The debate over banking reorganisation raged in Tokyo at the same time that a major transformation in official American policy toward Japan was occurring on the other side of the Pacific. Both Marquat and the Supreme Commander were strong supporters of the economic democratisation programme, yet the fluid political conditions of early 1948 made them wary of taking a firm position on banking reorganisation.[59]

During the first two years of occupation, the top policymakers in Washington took little notice of economic conditions and US Occupation policy in Japan, apparently assuming that MacArthur was effectively implementing the broad plans drawn up prior to the surrender.[60] By the end of 1947, however, influential officers in the State and Army Departments had begun to show interest in the

Japanese economy and SCAP administration. The flood of negative statistics and pessimistic forecasts pouring out of Tokyo increasingly worried those in Washington concerned with Asian affairs and the disbursement of foreign aid. Some, viewing the fall of China to the Communists as imminent, believed that action should be taken to rebuild Japan as a strong American ally in 'cold war' Asia. Others, noting Japan's sluggish industrial recovery, were concerned that Japan would become a permanent economic ward of the United States unless measures were taken immediately.

In effect, a new consensus on the proper role and orientation of MacArthur's Occupation emerged in Washington during 1947. In what some historians have critically labelled the 'reverse course', the American policymakers decided that SCAP's reform programmes should be de-emphasised, with more of the Occupation's energy focused on the economic rehabilitation of Japan. Those SCAP programmes that threatened economic recovery — like reparations, the promotion of organised labour and, in particular, deconcentration — were to be drastically reduced or altogether abandoned under this new policy orientation. Potentially disruptive democratisation schemes had no place in the revised American plan for Japan, which, in the words of Army Secretary Kenneth Royall, sought above all to build in Japan 'a self-supporting economy, strong enough and stable enough to support itself against any other totalitarian war threats which might hereafter arise in the Far East'.[61]

The individual most responsible for the implementation of the 'reverse course' in economic policy was Under Secretary of the Army William H. Draper, Jr. Tagged the 'Wall Street General', Draper had been a vice-president at the prestigious New York investment bank of Dillon Read before the war. Prior to his appointment as Under Secretary in 1947, he had served for two years as Chief Economic Advisor to General Lucius Clay in Germany, where he had assisted in the currency conversion and forcefully opposed a harsh antitrust policy against the *konzerns*. Draper was a shrewd, conservative financier, knowledgeable in economics and the ways of business, with little respect for 'idealistic' reformers or spendthrift bureaucrats. To Ted Cohen, and no doubt to others in SCAP who were committed to 'democratic' change, the Under Secretary appeared a 'practical [man] of affairs who dealt not in intangible hopes, concerns and aspirations but in money and the material things it stood for'.[62]

Draper first visited Japan in September of 1947 and found little there to his liking. Though critical of virtually all SCAP economic policy, Draper was particularly worried by the possible economic repercussions of the deconcentration programme SCAP was then pressing upon the Japanese. Indeed, the reformers' plans to reorganise Japan's industry and finance were, in the final months of 1947 and early 1948, to come under close scrutiny and forceful criticism from the United States. After *Newsweek* magazine carried a scathing report on SCAP's agenda for structural reform,[63] the deconcentration issue developed into a major public controversy in Washington. Secretary of Defense James Forrestal, another alumnus of Dillon Read, accused Edward Welsh of carrying out a 'social policy' which made it 'totally impossible for any business in Japan to plan for the future'.[64] Senator William Knowland, on learning of the provisions of SWNCC 302, vigorously condemned SCAP's deconcentration policies in Congress, stating, 'it is unbelievable to me that such a document would be put forward as representing the policy of the Government of which I am a part'.[65]

By the beginning of 1948, Draper and his colleagues in the Army and State Departments seem to have decided that SCAP's deconcentration programme would have to be scrapped, or, at the very least, drastically reduced in scope. To communicate Washington's position to MacArthur and his reformers, who were rather slow to appreciate the profound swing in American policy, Draper decided to lead a blue-ribbon mission of prominent persons to Japan in the spring. The mission was officially charged with investigating economic conditions in Japan, but Draper clearly intended to use his high-profile delegation to impress the changes in US policy upon the reformers of SCAP.

The Draper Mission was in Japan during March 1948 and met with the SCAP personnel and Japanese officials most concerned with economic policy. The members of the group, hand-picked by Draper, were conservative businessmen, inclined to oppose SCAP's economic reform programmes philosophically as well as on a purely practical basis. Bankers were well represented, as the five-man Mission included, in addition to Draper, Percy H. Johnston, Chairman of Chemical Bank, and Robert F. Loree, former Vice-President at Guaranty Trust Company.[66] Not surprisingly, therefore, while the Mission members were highly critical of the deconcentration policy as a whole, they seem to have shown particular concern over the banking question. Suspicious of the Antitrust Division's intentions and sympathetic to ESS-FI's more pragmatic stance, the Draper Mission sought to ensure that the Japanese financial system would not be forcibly deconcentrated by SCAP.[67]

The delegation was apparently successful in getting its message across to the Supreme Commander. Although MacArthur was philosophically committed to economic democratisation, he seems finally to have realised that the deconcentration programme was no longer acceptable to Washington and would require immediate modification. In discussions on antitrust policy, MacArthur assured the Mission that industrial deconcentration would be strictly limited to a small number of patently monopolistic firms and that financial institutions would not be structurally reformed. LeCount reported with clear satisfaction on 28 April that,

> Col. Baker [Civil Affairs Division, Department of the Army] explained that from discussions with members of the 'Draper Mission' he clearly understood that Gen. MacArthur indicated to members of the 'Draper Mission' that the banks would not be deconcentrated, and referred to the concurring views and understandings in this regard of Mr. Johnson [sic] and Mr. Loree, the banker members of the 'Draper Mission'. It was pointed out that Mr. Loree did not go into the steps which would be involved in breaking up the branch banks because he had understood such action was not to be taken and could not be taken without great injury to the banks involved, as well as the credit and other economic conditions of Japan.[68]

The Draper Mission's firm stand and MacArthur's assurances did not put an end to the ESS's internal debate over banking reform, however. While the Finance Division initially believed that the banks had been freed from any of Welsh's plans for democratisation, ESS-A/C remained committed to significant reorganisation of the financial system. General Marquat agreed with the Antitrust Division that some reform of the banking structure was necessary, though MacArthur had clearly ruled out any surgical operations on financial institutions. Thus, on 18 April, Marquat suggested that Welsh prepare a new reform programme which would dissolve the 'concentrations of financial power' without breaking up any banks or upsetting Japan's economic recovery.[69]

The Finance Division was quick to realise that the fight was not over and, hoping to gain leverage over Antitrust, submitted a hastily-prepared reform plan to Marquat on 23 April. ESS-FI proposed that the four *zaibatsu* banks and Sanwa be given 'preliminary designations' as excessive concentrations, but that this information not be made public. Each of these institutions would then be confidentially informed of this designation and presented with a list of financial and organisational reforms which they would be asked to comply with.

If the designated banks agreed to SCAP's conditions, a public announcement was to be made stating that the banks had completed voluntary reorganisations and would not be required to undergo American-imposed reform.[70]

The 'voluntary' reforms which the Finance Division proposed were virtually the same as the measures which had already been applied to all 'restricted concerns', including the major banks, under Ordinance 567. Those institutions given 'preliminary designations' were to be asked to break all affiliations with combine enterprises through stock ownership, personnel linkages and preferential credit ties. In addition, ESS-FI suggested requiring the banks to sever connections with the securities companies and increase their capital.[71] Overall, the list of conditions with which the designated banks were to comply was not particularly rigorous and did not hold the promise of significantly reducing the financial influence of the largest institutions. This scheme was obviously very attractive to the Finance Division, however, as it was sure to cause little disruption in the operations of the affected banks and, as no public designations were to be made, would not upset confidence in the financial system.

ESS-A/C gave the new Finance Division plan a predictably cool reception, questioning its basic approach and expressing doubts about the sufficiency of its proposed reforms. Welsh's primary objection was that the ESS-FI programme was based on 'secrecy and illegality' and that if sincere antitrust reform of the banks was still intended, then it had best be carried out in the public eye. The Antitrust Division thus suggested that the banks be formally designated as excessive concentrations by the HCLC and receive the same treatment as industrial firms to be reorganised under Law 207. The banks would not be forced to break up — the plan for establishing banking districts was totally abandoned — but they would be instructed to undertake internal reforms similar to, though much stricter than, those suggested by the ESS-FI programme.[72] Welsh maintained that the Finance Division plan would have had very little real effect on the power of the large banks and that further democratising reforms would be 'required and desirable'.[73]

Despite the Antitrust criticisms, Marquat reacted favourably to the ESS-FI plan and, after confirming its legality with the SCAP lawyers,[74] instructed Welsh and LeCount to proceed along those lines. Marquat vacillated, however, informing the Division Chiefs on 14 May that under no circumstances would the banks be exempted from designation under Law 207, thus seeming to espouse the ESS-A/C counterproposal.[75] The General is reported to have informed

Finance Minister Kitamura at the same time that the financial institutions would indeed be subject to the provisions of the Deconcentration Law.[76] Less than two weeks later, however, Marquat's position had once again reversed, as he proposed in a memorandum to the Chief of Staff that,

> No structural reorganization of financial institutions will be required in the sense of increasing the number of independent banking institutions or insurance companies through division of existing organizations. This finding is in accordance with the conclusions reached by the Draper mission . . . Banks and insurance companies will not be subject to designation under the provisions of the 'Elimination of Excessive Concentrations of Economic Power Law'.[77]

Marquat's swing back to a more lenient stand on the banking issue may well have been influenced by his superiors. Early in May, Draper sent the Supreme Commander an informal report prepared by an unidentified American banker who had recently returned from a business trip in Japan. Draper expressed admiration for the short paper, which concluded firmly that 'extensive decentralization in the fields of banking and insurance would be most unwise'.[78] Though hardly a major pronouncement on American policy, this sharp little message from Draper may have galvanised MacArthur and Marquat to seek a final solution to the banking question.[79]

As the Finance and Antitrust Divisions still could not resolve their differences, the upper echelons of SCAP were forced to look elsewhere for a simple, immediate resolution to the banking reform debate. By the early summer, MacArthur and Marquat appear to have been searching for a face-saving way out of the banking deconcentration tangle. They eventually decided to submit the issue to the Deconcentration Review Board (DRB), an American panel charged with screening the reorganisation of firms under Law 207. The Board had been originally proposed by MacArthur at the height of the deconcentration controversy in Washington to appease critics of SCAP antitrust policy. Draper subsequently saw the DRB as a convenient tool for limiting the imposition of Law 207 and appointed as its members conservative businessmen critical of SCAP's reformist policy. During its tenure in Japan from May 1948 to August 1949, the DRB did as Draper had planned, neutralising SCAP's deconcentration programme by ruling that the vast majority of designated industrial enterprises (314 out of a total 325) would be spared forced structural reorganisation.

The Review Board's pronouncement on the banking issue was no doubt very satisfying to Draper and those members of the Occupation who shared his commitment to economic reconstruction. On 2 July 1948, the DRB informed the Supreme Commander,

> In the Board's opinion, it is not necessary under existing conditions and it is inadvisable to break up the Yasuda, Teikoku [Mitsui], Mitsubishi, Sanwa and Sumitomo banks . . . Breaking up these banks would be almost certain to cause a loss of public confidence. Division of these banks would produce a group of smaller banks, the deposits in each of which would be insufficient to serve adequately the loan requirements of large borrowers . . . Moreover, each of these banks is now under-capitalized and is faced with the necessity of raising additional equity capital. A break-up would increase the difficulties of attracting this capital.[80]

The DRB concluded that the maintenance of competition in the financial sector was assured under the legal provisions of the Antimonopoly Law and the responsible, permanent surveillance of the newly established Fair Trade Commission.[81]

To MacArthur and Marquat, the DRB decision was the final word on the bank deconcentration question. Welsh, however, tenaciously continued the fight, still recommending, even after the DRB pronouncement, that the banks be designated by the HCLC.[82] As the antitrust programmes collapsed under the accelerating 'reverse course', however, Welsh became increasingly embattled in his position as SCAP's leading economic reformer. Finally, he was forced to recognise defeat on the banking deconcentration issue. In a personal note of 18 July to General Marquat, Welsh confided that his health had been broken by the events of the past months and that he was at last ready to admit that the fight was over:

> Let me briefly refer to . . . the 'bank question'. I'm damned if I know why there has been so much confusion and emotion about it. I made various proposals for carrying out what the facts caused me to propose honestly and objectively. When I grasped, and perhaps I was slow to catch on, that a decision had been made at higher levels to the effect that the banks were not to be reorganized under the Deconcentration Law, I accepted that decision and proposed a series of different methods for handling the decision. At no time was there fair basis for questioning my motives or my knowledge of the laws or economic factors involved.[83]

Thus, with the debate inside SCAP finally stilled, all that remained was to publicise the official decision on the reorganisation of the Japanese banks. Welsh drafted a press release based closely on the DRB document and presented it to the HCLC, which duly accepted it.[84] With the Commission's public announcement on 31 July 1948, after more than six months of often bitter dispute within SCAP and across the Pacific, the 'bank question' was at last given a final answer.

In the end, SCAP's antitrust programme had an almost negligible effect on the Japanese banks. The recovery of the financial system was perhaps impeded by the uncertainty which surrounded the application of Law 207, yet, as the largest banks were not designated as holding companies or forcibly dissolved, the democratisation programmes directly caused little disruption in the rehabilitation of Japanese finance. The 'preferential' treatment given to the banks was largely due to the efforts of ESS-FI, whose dedication to financial reconstruction led it to oppose reform efforts which would jeopardise the recovery. As a State Department analysis of the *zaibatsu* programme concluded,

> Except insofar as regulations of general application may have affected the banks, nothing has been done with respect to the existing enormous concentrations of assets in a few Japanese banks. This has been due partly to the fact that the problem of deconcentration as it relates to banks has rested in the Finance Division of SCAP rather than in the . . . Antitrust Division. The former Division has been primarily preoccupied with the technical aspects of bank operations and, understandably enough, has been inimical to any program which might disturb the *status quo*.[85]

The frustration of antitrust reform in banking can be traced directly to the bureaucratic rift which developed between Welsh and his ESS-FI colleagues. What began as a difference of opinion became — as a result of poor administrative co-ordination, 'feudal' rivalries and the confusion surrounding the 'reverse course' — a seemingly irreconcilable clash of jurisdictions, personalities and outlooks. The Occupation's muddled organisation and cluttered chain of command — with independent missions, numerous Washington agencies, the Supreme Commander and the many factions of the SCAP bureaucracy vying for a say in American policy — made the smooth and rapid settlement of internal disputes virtually impossible. As SCAP's experience in banking deconcentration shows, inter-divisional disagreements over priorities, methods or jurisdiction could lead to bureaucratic paralysis and the stagnation of reform. The Finance Division's persistent opposition to deconcentration snarled the planning process, stalled the reformers' initiatives and ultimately overcame the 'trust busters'' resolve. In the end, it seems that bureaucratic infighting rather than 'reverse course' re-evaluation was the critical factor in derailing Welsh's designs for structural reorganisation in finance. Indeed, the shift in Washington's policy did not so much 'reverse' plans for banking reform as merely hasten Welsh's acceptance of what ESS-FI opposition had already made inevitable: the abandonment of heavy-handed banking deconcentration as impracticable, unnecessary and economically ill-advised.

Although the 'bank question' was seemingly put to rest in 1948, the issue flared once more during the Occupation, very unexpectedly and publicly. On 2 March 1950, at the 108th meeting of the Allied Council for Japan, a multi-national advisory committee, the Australian representative Colonel W.R. Hodgson brought up the issue of concentration and *zaibatsu* control in banking. Arguing that eight banks dominated '80% of the industrial and economic life of this country', Hodgson demanded an investigation into why SCAP had not deconcentrated the financial sector. Ambassador William Sebald, the American representative and chairman, immediately ordered the remarks stricken from the official record as a breach of procedure. Nevertheless, Hodgson's outburst found its way into the press and the banking reform issue was re-opened, much to SCAP's annoyance.[86]

The situation was exacerbated by a report in the *Nippon Times* of 10 March 1950 that Edward Welsh, still Chief of the ESS-A/C, had announced to a group of Osaka businessmen that SCAP was planning action to 'break up the domination of banks over Japanese industrial activity'.[87] Welsh steadfastly denied ever making these comments but clearly indicated to his superiors that he still bore ill-will over the final resolution of the banking question:

> My views, as well as those of the Supreme Commander, regarding the non-exemption of Zaibatsu banks from the Deconcentration Law had become public knowledge a long time ago. However, once the decision was made that banks were not to be designated, I have refrained from any public utterance which could properly be interpreted as criticizing such decision.[88]

There was little sympathy for Welsh's views in SCAP or amongst the Japanese public, however. Marquat drafted a press release in response to Hodgson's allegations and the statement attributed to

Welsh, curtly dismissing the reform efforts of 1947–8 yet maintaining that banking had been successfully democratised:

> It was the unanimous decision of [the DRB] that it would be most destructive to attempt a fragmentation of the large banks involved merely upon a basis of the size of the individual corporate unit. Further, it was indicated as the consensus of the board that it would be folly compounded to attempt to impose upon the Japanese banking system any academic reforms which have remained unproven throughout the world.[89]

Marquat's statement put an end to the renewed interest in the banking deconcentration issue. By 1950, with the Japanese economy turning up and the American Occupation winding down, the antitrust programmes of the past were only a distant memory. The rejection of reformist 'idealism' and heavy-handed democratisation which had begun in 1947 was apparently complete, as Japanese commercial banking, though little changed structurally since the surrender, was publicly endorsed by SCAP as competitive and progressive. The Occupation never willingly admitted its own deficiencies and thus, in the end, SCAP neatly reinterpreted the collapse of its banking deconcentration efforts as a victory for the American mission in Japan.

4

Legal Reform of the Financial System, 1948–50

Although the Finance Division vehemently resisted Welsh's attempts to deconcentrate Japanese commercial banking, LeCount and his subordinates were not opposed to economic democratisation in principle. In the 1948 debate, ESS-FI raised objections to the Antitrust Division's banking programme on practical grounds, but offered no criticism of the reformers' aim of promoting in Japan a competitive, 'democratic' economic structure. The personnel of the Finance Division seem not to have questioned the need for banking reform, only the approach to it which their colleagues in Antitrust and Cartels had adopted.

Indeed, from early in the Occupation, ESS-FI had been independently exploring alternative programmes for the democratisation of Japan's financial system. Approaching the 'bank question' with characteristic pragmatism and concern for the wider implications of financial policy, the planners of the Finance Division had by 1948 developed a series of reforms designed to democratise without debilitating the banks or upsetting economic recovery in the process. Working with different assumptions and priorities than their colleagues in Antitrust, yet striving for the same ultimate goal, the bureaucrats of ESS-FI devised a proposal for financial reform which bore little resemblance to Welsh's grand plan for banking deconcentration.

In brief outline, the Finance Division's democratisation programme comprised two distinct though complementary stages of reform. First, the Occupation was to foster competition within the existing banking structure, primarily by promoting non-*zaibatsu* institutions to challenge the financial superiority of the largest banks. Secondly, SCAP was to ensure long-term adherence to democratic principles by establishing clear legal codes of practice for the banking industry and reorganising government financial administration to provide for the even-handed and rigorous enforcement of the new regulations. Clearly, the Finance Division scheme was founded on the belief that by creating powerful countervailing forces — in the form of stringent legislation, vigilant watchdogs and viable new competitors — the rise of a banking oligopoly and the resurgence of a dictatorial financial bureaucracy could be prevented in postwar Japan.

During the 1948 banking debate, the ESS-FI plan emerged as a viable counter-proposal to the Antitrust Division's reform initiative. On the basis of the two-stage programme, LeCount and his subordinates argued that a thorough, long-term democratisation of Japan's financial sector was possible without resorting to the drastic, destructive measures recommended by Edwards and Welsh. Nevertheless, the rejection of banking deconcentration by Washington and its proxies did not signify official endorsement of the Finance Division plan. Rather, once the bureaucratic furore surrounding the Antitrust proposal had subsided, the ESS-FI scheme, and in particular the provision for legal reform, became the centre of a renewed debate over SCAP banking policy.

The first stage of the Finance Division plan, pursued quietly, gradually and without clear official sanction from 1947 until the end of the Occupation, aimed at promoting increased competition within the existing banking structure, amongst the existing institutions. The intention was to induce competition organically rather than to establish it artificially, to further economic democracy through a constructive process rather than by forced deconcentration. In sum, the planners of the Finance Division held that the optimal method of fostering broad financial competition and simultaneously strengthening the banking system was by fortifying the weaker institutions, not by penalising the stronger. Thus, rejecting the Antitrust proposal for fragmenting the *zaibatsu* banks as destructive and ultimately unnecessary, ESS-FI worked to encourage the development of prefectural, savings and trust banks as viable, assertive rivals of the entrenched *zaibatsu* institutions.

The bureaucrats of the Finance Division recognised that with the dislocations of defeat, both the need for rehabilitation and the potential for introducing democratic change were great. While the *zaibatsu* and governmental financial institutions had been most deeply involved in the war effort and commanded the lion's share of SCAP's reformist attention, all elements of Japanese finance were profoundly affected by the defeat and thus subjected to ESS-FI scrutiny. The prefectural banks, for example, were not as committed to industrial or government financing as their urban counterparts, but were nevertheless comparably weak and structurally unsound following the surrender. The savings banks were in an even more precarious state, their business ruined by wartime regulations, the spiralling inflation and the accompanying shrinkage in personal deposits. The trust banks, although linked to the *zaibatsu* organisations, also faced an uncertain future, as defeat had left them stranded with virtually worthless investments and few prospects for recovery in the bleak postwar environment. The agricultural co-operatives, commercial credit associations and related financial organs, which had suffered extensive official manipulation during the war, were confronted with equally dismal circumstances.[1]

The Finance Division sought to redirect and strengthen these various ailing institutions in their transition to a peacetime economy. The four savings banks, lacking a clear role in the postwar financial world, were converted to or merged with commercial banks during 1947 and 1948. The six trust banks were also reorganised under ESS-FI leadership and were allowed to combine commercial banking business with their normal investment activities. The prefectural banks did not require such major reconstruction but the Finance Division encouraged their growth by promoting their expansion into regional operations. The co-operatives and credit associations were released from wartime regulations, reorganised and enabled to diversify their services.[2]

The Americans also acted to spur competition when the commercial banks were allowed to re-enter the field of international finance. Thus, when in 1948 the Japanese government recommended that the eight large 'city banks'[3] be the only institutions designated 'Class A' foreign exchange banks, and hence the only institutions able to establish correspondent relations overseas, the Finance Division balked. ESS-FI insisted that the list be expanded to twelve, adding the Kobe, Daiwa, Tokai and Nippon Kangyo Banks to increase competition in foreign trade financing and simultaneously to bolster the domestic prestige of the four additional institutions. The Finance Division also encouraged the establishment of a 'Class B' designation which afforded the larger prefectural banks and the reorganised trust banks some valuable, albeit limited, exposure to international operations.[4]

In general, the Finance Division's efforts seemed less a broad, co-ordinated initiative for change than a patchwork of seemingly minor and unrelated financial reforms. Nevertheless, by working consistently to induce increased competition when practicable, the bureaucrats of

ESS-FI managed to attain significant results both in terms of democratic change and economic rehabilitation. The prefectural banks, buoyed by Finance Division support for expansion in domestic operations and international involvement, recovered steadily and developed into active competitors of the city banks in certain fields. The credit co-operatives capitalised on the opportunities opened by SCAP reorganisation and enjoyed unprecedented growth in the postwar decades. The savings and trust banks were salvaged under American supervision, the revitalised institutions ultimately assuming an active role in Japanese finance and providing increased competition in commercial banking.[5]

The Finance Division's success in implementing these varied reforms was notable considering the complications so frequently encountered in the pursuit of SCAP financial policy. Significantly, the ESS-FI efforts provoked little controversy, either from the Japanese government, the banks themselves or from within SCAP. By managing to induce competition and support financial reconstruction simultaneously, the Finance programmes seem to have satisfied both the reformers in the ESS and the most economically concerned among the Japanese. As Tristan Beplat has noted, however, the importance of bureaucratic politics to the Divison's success in implementation should not be underestimated:

Matters such as reorganizing the banks . . . establishing trust and banking corporations, and designating foreign-exchange banks, apparently were considered to be purely banking matters, and with regard to them the Finance Division developed its own policies without any interference.[6]

Thus the Finance Division seems to have achieved, at least in 'purely banking matters', what Harry Emerson Wildes termed a 'private empire', controlling the planning and implementation of SCAP policy in a specific sphere of influence which was recognised and respected by the various sectors of the American bureaucracy.[7] So long as it stayed within its 'empire' and did not encroach upon other bureaucratic enclaves, ESS-FI was apparently able to follow programmes of its own design without inciting potentially paralysing internal conflict. With a sheltered 'fief' in the 'feudal' structure of SCAP, undistracted by bureaucratic jealousies and internecine skirmishes, the Finance Division enjoyed uncommon ease in pursuing its uncommonly consistent and successful range of constructive banking reforms.

In the final analysis, the ESS-FI policies might not have delivered rapid results or guaranteed a 'democratic' structure in Japanese banking, but they did serve to broaden the base of competition and strengthen the weakest elements of the financial sector. Although by the standards of the Antitrust Division the programme was unambitious and its results limited, the Finance Division's patchwork reforms coalesce in retrospect into a considerable effort for fostering constructive competition and healthy rivalry in the Japanese banking sector. Some limited democratising reform was possible, it seems, without inflicting dire side-effects upon the reconstruction of the financial system or the greater economic revival.

The Finance Division recognised from the beginning, however, that the programme of inducing competition, no matter how broad or successful, was not comprehensive and could not alone assure the long-term democratisation of Japanese finance. While the planners of ESS-FI recognised their success in nurturing competitive forces in the banking system, they believed that these new 'democratic' energies would almost certainly be stifled under the existing legal and administrative framework. Thus, a second stage of reform was considered essential to the attainment of lasting, meaningful change in Japan's financial hierarchy. Going beyond Antitrust deconcentration proposals and its own efforts to promote competition, the Finance Division looked to establishing permanent statutes and regulatory organisations which would uphold and maintain democratic standards in Japanese banking even after the occupiers had departed.

The Finance Division reforms were based on an understanding of current conditions and an interpretation of historical developments in the financial system which differed fundamentally from the Antitrust Division's view. To ESS-FI, the *zaibatsu* banks were not the bogeymen of the Japanese financial world, for they as institutions were not responsible for the 'undemocratic' development of the banking structure. Rather, the planners of the Finance Division saw the *zaibatsu* banks as the products of a flawed system — the government's legal barriers and administrative controls — and not the producers of it. LeCount and his subordinates attributed the 'un-American' development of the financial sector to prewar and wartime government policy which had consistently discriminated against some institutions (such as prefectural and savings banks) so as to bolster the development of others (particularly the *zaibatsu* banks) as instruments of government policy. The authorities had sacrificed competition and sound banking practices to attain their authoritarian, militaristic goals. Thus, the Finance Division maintained that the laws and institutions designed to control and distort the evolution of the financial system, and not those banks which had profited from government favouritism, were the 'undemocratic' cancer that had to be removed by SCAP.

With this interpretation, the planners of ESS–FI plainly rejected forced deconcentration as a futile attack on the symptoms rather than an adequate solution to the deeper causes of the 'undemocratic' development of Japanese finance. Competition could be promoted within the existing system, but unless the legal basis of banking was altered, the pre-surrender pattern of direct, politically motivated control could easily be reasserted through the existing regulatory channels. Thus, ESS–FI proposed a major democratisation, in essence an 'Americanisation', of Japanese banking law, hoping to introduce in Japan fair and sound codes of practice and responsible, apolitical organs for enforcing them. The implicit assumption was that such legal reform would lead inevitably to the liberation of competitive forces in the private sector, the transformation of banking operations and, in the end, to a pervasive 'Americanisation' of the entire system.

From the beginning of the Occupation, the Finance Division and other elements in SCAP recognised that the legal and regulatory under-pinnings of Japanese finance would have to be evaluated in light of American goals and postwar economic realities. As early as 1946, considerable interest was being shown in the reform of banking laws, and various preliminary ideas for change were under discussion. From the start of such investigations, there seems to have been a general consensus among the concerned planners in SCAP that governmental administration of the financial sector would have to be reorganised, with a clear role assigned to the Bank of Japan and the extensive powers of the Ministry of Finance limited. The occupiers also seemed to agree that strengthened procedures of bank examination and clear legal provisions against 'undemocratic' practices such as interlocking directorates should be established.

The first major policy document to discuss the issue of legal reforms in finance was the 1946 report prepared by the Edwards Mission. In their study of the *zaibatsu*, the American experts briefly evaluated the role of the government in the prewar rise of the combine banks. The report concluded that the central authorities had supported the development of an oligopolistic financial structure by clearly favouring the interests of the *zaibatsu* institutions in matters such as merger policy, branching regulations and bank examinations.[8] Such blatant discrimination was only possible, the paper maintained, because of the distorted legal framework of Japanese finance:

Japanese financial laws follow a common pattern. They prescribe

73

certain general standards with respect to the institutions they purport to regulate and vest absolute power in the Minister of Finance to define, alter, and enforce the standards. In reality, they place no serious limitations upon the minister's power.[9]

Edwards and his associates, however, viewed the *zaibatsu* organisations, and not the militarist administration, as being fundamentally responsible for Japan's 'undemocratic' economic development. Thus, evidence of government favouritism toward the combine banks was used by Edwards to show that the Ministry of Finance was a tool of *zaibatsu* interests. Legal reform of banking was therefore considered far less important than breaking the *zaibatsu* organisations and purging their supporters from positions of responsibility. Indeed, in its final recommendations, the Edwards Mission did not call for major reforms of banking laws or government regulation, only offering the suggestions that

> The discretion which the laws now entrust to the Minister of Finance should be greatly reduced. Bank examinations should take place at least every two years . . . All vestiges of private ownership of the Bank of Japan should be eliminated.[10]

The recommendations of the Edwards Mission on legal change in banking were accepted without objection by SCAP-GHQ and the Antitrust Division[11] and ultimately were incorporated into SWNCC 302 with only minor amplifications.[12] Nevertheless, the personnel of ESS-A/C and the reformist elements in Washington initially exhibited little interest in pursuing any such programme of legal reorganisation. Presumably, the Antitrust Division, continually over-extended with various projects, considered the proposed reform of financial laws either too minor or too narrowly technical a matter for its immediate attention. Thus, as the 'trust busters' did not undertake any planning on the restructuring of banking laws and administration, the full responsibility for this line of democratisation policy fell to the Finance Division.[13]

ESS-FI accepted the reform of government financial regulation as its province and began an extensive study of possible legal change in 1946. The planning effort was established in the Special Projects Unit of the Money and Banking Branch under the leadership of C.E. Cagle, a senior analyst from the US Federal Reserve Board on loan to SCAP. Cagle was one of several American specialists in central banking and financial law who were supplied by the Federal Reserve to developing countries in need of expert assistance on governmental regulation of finance. In the first years following the war, this American technical aid was in wide demand and was responsible for the development of general banking acts and central bank laws in countries from Guatemala to the Philippines. In Japan, as elsewhere, the charge of the legal architects was to design a system adapted to local financial needs and conditions yet still able to ensure high standards of stability and fair competition in the banking sector.[14]

Cagle's planning proceeded slowly, however, and for more than two years no papers on the legal reform of banking were circulated outside the Finance Division. By mid-1947, a year after the establishment of the Special Projects Unit, the scope and direction of ESS-FI's reform were apparently quite well defined, although the drafting of actual legislation had not yet begun. Cagle and his associates were clearly looking beyond the unambitious reforms which Edwards had proposed to a full revision of banking laws and a fundamental reorganisation of government regulation. In a report to the Allied Council in April 1947, Tristan Beplat gave a hint of the institutional reforms which ESS-FI planned to introduce:

> The Bank of Japan will continue in its present role as the central bank, being charged with the issue of the national currency. Within the limitations of credit policies and currency limitation to be determined by a committee of cabinet level, it will continue to make loans and re-discounts to other banks . . . It is contemplated that the stock ownership of this bank will pass from present combination of governmental and private ownership to joint ownership by various financial institutions.[15]

The impetus to finalise plans for legal reform was provided by the disclosure of the Antitrust Division's scheme to 'neutralise' the *zaibatsu* banks by partition. To bolster its opposition to Welsh's democratisation proposal, the Finance Division needed to offer the higher authorities a viable alternative to forced deconcentration. Although Cagle's research was not yet complete, LeCount and his associates apparently thought it imperative to introduce the legal reform counter-proposal as rapidly as possible and to present it as a non-destructive, practical and effective option for the democratic reform of banking. The object was to convince Marquat, MacArthur and the powers in Washington that the fragmentation of the *zaibatsu* banks was unnecessary, its crippling side-effects avoidable and yet permanent democratisation of finance attainable under ESS–FI's planned legal reforms.

Thus, on 8 March 1948, one month after the release of Welsh's deconcentration proposal, the Finance Division informed General Marquat that it was well advanced in the preparation of a comprehensive banking reform programme, incorporating a revision of the general banking law, a reorganisation of the Bank of Japan and the establishment of an independent board to supervise the financial sector. LeCount reported that the proposed initiative would include 'many tangible corrective features and prohibitions designed to destroy monopolistic positions . . . and to aid in the establishment of free enterprises which will be rid of any undesirable concentration of power'.[16] The memorandum concluded with the confident claim that 'such a program should effectively eliminate any actual excessive concentration of economic power by the banks or prevent this occurrence thereof' without resorting to the drastic measures proposed by the Antitrust Division.[17]

The memorandum of 8 March gave simply a broad outline of Cagle's plan and essentially only affirmed ESS–FI's intention to introduce an extensive counter-proposal to the deconcentration programme. Not until 28 May, following consultations with Antitrust and members of the Draper Mission, did the Finance Division circulate a detailed exposition of its proposed legal reform for discussion within SCAP. In a 22-page memorandum from LeCount to Marquat, the conclusions of two years' research by Cagle were carefully outlined and systematically explained. With the release of this significant planning document, the Finance Division finally presented a concrete challenge to Welsh's democratisation initiative.

LeCount's memorandum did not include a draft of the new law which the planners envisaged, but rather introduced a list of detailed provisions which were intended to form the basis of legal reform. ESS–FI did not plan to turn this outline into a full draft internally, suggesting instead that the recommendations should be communicated to the Japanese, who could then take responsibility for writing the suitable legislation under SCAP supervision.[18] The Finance Division had originally planned to prepare a complete draft law to present to the Japanese for ratification;[19] however, apparently in haste to put the basic proposal forward, and also perhaps in the hope of effecting a less heavy-handed reform, LeCount abandoned this time-consuming and imperious approach.

The Finance Division memorandum recommended a new overall banking law to replace the existing statutes governing bank operations and practices, the organisation and functions of the Bank of Japan and the determination of monetary policy and credit control. The ESS–FI proposal focused on three central provisions which Cagle saw as the basis for the legal revisions and administrative alterations that would ensure lasting change in Japanese banking.

First, the Finance Division's legislative plan called for the establishment of a 'Banking Board' with Cabinet rank, independent of partisan and bureaucratic influences and vested with broad powers. In short, the plan sought to break the political manipulation of financial development by establishing a new, autonomous power-centre in the Japanese government with full responsibility for the regulation of banking and a commitment to sound democratic principles. The memorandum described this new agency as

A Board whose members are experienced in banking, finance, commerce, and agriculture, and inexperienced in politics . . . [which] will be responsible for the formulation and enforcement of all monetary and credit policies of the Government and will regulate and supervise all banks and all other credit and financial institutions, within limits fixed by law sufficiently comprehensive and definite to afford reasonable protection against undue domination or dictatorship over banks by the Government.[20]

The proposed Board was to have seven full-time members, nominated by the Prime Minister and approved by the Diet, who were to be 'selected with a view to geographical and institutional or functional representation'.[21] The members would be appointed for unrenewable fourteen-year terms, staggered to promote continuity, and would receive salaries at the highest level of the public-service pay scale. All the Board members were to be given equal voting rights in committee, with a chairman named from among the members by the Prime Minister.

The independence of the Banking Board from established bureaucratic and political interests was of prime importance, and Cagle sought to guarantee autonomy through organisational arrangements. Politicians were to be expressly excluded from Board membership and the memorandum suggested the inclusion of some legal restrictions 'to prevent undue domination [of the Board] by any of the political parties'.[22] The proposed Board was to answer only to the Diet, not to the Cabinet or the Finance Ministry. Nevertheless, to promote communication and policy co-ordination with the central government, the chairman was to be created an *ex officio* member of the Cabinet and encouraged to 'counsel with the Minister of Finance' on issues of financial and economic policy.[23]

Cagle's proposal assigned broad and substantial authority to the new Banking Board, in essence transferring to it the extensive powers in financial and monetary policy then being exercised by the Minister of Finance. The Board's primary responsibility was to 'formulate and administer national monetary and credit policies in the public interest', for which it was to be given the authority to determine

> . . . loan and discount rates, margin requirements, reserves, interest rates on deposits, limits on loans secured by stocks and bonds and the rates of interest on such loans, as a means of regulating speculative securities, etc., and various open market operations.[24]

In addition, the Board was to assume 'overall responsibility for the administration of law with respect to the regulation and supervision of the various financial institutions', including sole governmental responsibility for chartering banks, approving mergers, regulating branching and conducting bank examinations. Finally, the Board was to undertake economic research and the collection, analysis and publication of pertinent financial information.

Cagle was, in effect, recommending the reorganisation of the government financial hierarchy along familiar American lines, with the new Banking Board essentially a streamlined version of the Board of Governors of the Federal Reserve System.[25] In many aspects of structure and function — from its research role to the tenure of its members — the Japanese Board was envisaged as a virtual carbon copy of its American counterpart. Significantly, however, Cagle sought to endow the Board with greater powers and responsibilities than the Federal Reserve, placing its chairman in the Cabinet and assigning the Board sole supervisory authority over all financial institutions. Cagle's proposed committee was thus an 'improved' model of the Board of Governors, as he sought to clarify some of the ambiguities and correct some of the perceived weaknesses in the Federal Reserve structure by assigning the Banking Board unequivocal statutory independence and unified supervisory control.[26]

The second central provision of the Finance Division reform plan, like the first, called for structural reorganisation in the Japanese government on an American model. Cagle sought, in the new banking legislation, to provide for

> Reorganization of the Bank of Japan, with a board of directors

selected from various areas of Japan and from various fields of [the] Japanese economy and with a corps of officers and employees responsible to the board of directors. The Bank will act as banker for the Japanese Government and the private banks. It will hold reserves of the banks, rediscount loans, operate a system of check clearing collections . . . handle bond issues, redemptions, and other fiscal operations.[27]

Cagle intended the Bank of Japan to be remodelled in the form of a Federal Reserve district bank, operating on a national scale, but otherwise with virtually identical structure, function and relation to the higher monetary authorities. The Finance Division proposed that the Bank be re-chartered as a reserve institution and its ownership pass fully into private hands, the new capital stock to be subscribed by all the Japanese banks.[28] As in the Federal Reserve System, the shareholders would only be entitled to a fixed annual return but would have a voice in the management of the Bank through a newly established, representative Board of Directors. The proposed Board, which would replace the impotent existing directorate,[29] organisationally mirrored that of a Federal Reserve Bank, with nine members serving three-year terms, three of the directors to be appointed by the Banking Board and the other six chosen by the stockholders, with some provisions for balanced geographical distribution. By establishing this new Board of Directors and transferring to it the responsibilities and powers which were, at the time, vested entirely in the Governor, the ESS–FI planners were confident they could introduce democratic methods and values into the Bank of Japan's structure and operations.[30]

The duties and prerogatives of the Bank in monetary operations were to be little changed in the proposed reform, although the establishment of the mandatory reserve system would have given the institution a new instrument of control. The Bank was to be removed, however, from the domination of the Ministry of Finance and clearly linked with the new Banking Board, their relationship to be essentially the same as that between the Board of Governors and the district Reserve Banks in the United States. In short, the Bank of Japan was to have no policymaking role but was to be charged only with implementing the programmes determined by the Banking Board. Cagle sought to end the long-standing enmity between the Governor and the Finance Minister by designing legislation which would clearly recognise the Banking Board as the architect and the Bank as the builder of Japanese monetary policy. Thus, in essence, the Bank of

79

Japan was to remain subservient, though to a different and — so Cagle promised — more democratic and responsible authority.

Finally, LeCount's memorandum turned to the proposed new general banking law and outlined the provisions which ESS–FI sought to see included in it. The recommendations put forward were highly detailed and, though not presented in a legally comprehensive form, appeared to address all aspects of the planned legislation thoroughly. Cagle's care in this area was apparent, for his aim was to introduce 'a bank law which incorporates as far as practicable, definite provisions as to what the banks can and cannot do, leaving as little as possible to arbitrary dictation from the Government'.[31] Cagle, an expert in such legislation, hoped to establish in the law principles of fair competition, free enterprise and sound operations which would govern the future, non-politicised development of Japanese finance.

The proposal placed great emphasis on 'democratising' provisions which, Cagle maintained, would prevent the rise of any postwar zaibatsu-like combines centred on commercial banks. Under the plan, the financial institutions were to be prohibited from forming any affiliations with industrial firms, forbidden to maintain personnel links with other enterprises through interlocking directorates and barred from establishing ties with securities companies or dealing directly in securities.[32] Furthermore, the volume of loans to individual firms was to be strictly limited to a fixed percentage of total loans, both to protect against the use of financial ties to exercise anti-competitive control and to guard depositors against unsound dependent relationships.

Cagle was as interested in guaranteeing the stability and safety of commercial banking with the new law as he was in using it to promote democratisation. The proposal detailed numerous restrictions on loan and investment policy, generally seeking to promote conservative business practices in banking. The need for an adequate and stable capital stock, a concern of ESS–FI since the beginning of the Occupation, was emphasised. Strict and precise rules were given on internal procedures, such as the conduct of shareholders' meetings, the organisation of bank management and the payment of dividends. Finally, the memorandum recommended the establishment of strong penalties, from removal from office to fines and imprisonment, for violations of the banking statutes.[33]

The Finance Division's outline of legal reform, released at the height of the debate over banking deconcentration, was viewed circumspectly by the Antitrust Division. Welsh's immediate reaction was to support the legislative efforts in principle, but to question some specific provisions of the proposal and its potential for democratisation.[34] Though lacking the technical knowledge to appraise Cagle's work adequately, the planners of ESS–A/C were not convinced that legal reform was a substitute for forced deconcentration, preferring to regard it simply as a supportive adjunct. An Antitrust Division report on banking reorganisation stated:

> It is certain that breaking the banks . . . will complete the job of the dissolution of Zaibatsu insofar as this is practicable through Occupation action. Adequate banking regulation, on the other hand, can provide no such assurance. Without adequate enforcement of such banking regulation nothing at all will be accomplished . . . In presupposing adequate enforcement of banking regulation, the A/C Division believes that the Finance Division is unduly optimistic . . . The Zaibatsu have successfully defied all regulations interfering with their privileges except those imposed by direct Occupation intervention. This being true, it is reasonable to assume that adequate enforcement of banking regulations will be accomplished only if carried out by Occupation personnel.[35]

Nevertheless, with the official rejection of banking deconcentration in July 1948, the Antitrust Division expressed increased support for the proposed legal reforms, despite lingering reservations.[36] The planners of ESS–FI, further buoyed by encouragement from several Washington officials,[37] thus proceeded with their legal planning, apparently under the assumption that the defeat of the Antitrust plan assured the official acceptance of their alternative scheme. On 15 July, LeCount submitted to General Marquat the draft of a memorandum to Prime Minister Ashida, which advised him to initiate the revision of banking laws in accordance with Cagle's plan.[38] The Finance Division anticipated ready approval, and Marquat was prepared to transmit it to the Japanese, but decided first to seek clearance from the Supreme Commander. MacArthur, apparently wary of initiating any new reforms, insisted that the higher authorities in Washington be consulted before further action was taken on legislative revision.[39]

By August 1948, when the ESS–FI forwarded Cagle's proposal to the Army Department, the 'reverse course' was well advanced in Washington and, as MacArthur had appreciated, 'democratic' reform of any type was looked upon rather suspiciously. Draper had successfully installed economic rehabilitation as the official focus of Occupation policy and had subsequently turned his attention to formulating the specific measures which would drive Japan's recovery. The Under

Secretary, with the sound analysis of a banker, concluded that the greatest hindrance to Japan's industrial revival was the rampaging inflation, which had yet to be brought under control by SCAP. Draper and his advisors believed that only with stability were true growth, overseas trade recovery and eventual Japanese economic independence possible.[40] Thus, with this orientation, the policymakers of Washington evaluated the Finance Division's reform proposals primarily on the basis of their possible impact on the stabilisation of the Japanese economy.

Draper, after consulting the State Department, Treasury and Federal Reserve, cabled SCAP on 27 October with 'tentative general comments and questions' on the legal reform programme, promising that a more detailed evaluation would follow at a later date. Though Draper reported 'general agreement here with your objective of establishing new and more independent monetary authority', the cable was not encouraging, advising SCAP to re-evaluate its proposals and move cautiously. Specific issues, such as the proposed Cabinet membership for the Banking Board chairman, were identified as being of concern in Washington. Draper, however, was clearly most interested in the broader economic implications of the legal reform:

> Principal concern here is that the success of such basic monetary and central banking reform would be jeopardized if introduced in present inflationary period before other fundamental measures are taken to stabilize the Japanese economy. Danger reform would become discredited by being associated with conditions for which it was not responsible. View here is that establishment new monetary authority should be integrated part of coordinated stabilization program and should be introduced only after program's success is reasonably assured.[41]

The Under Secretary appeared more concerned about the progress of the stabilisation programme than the benefits of democratisation and banking solidity which the proposed law promised, concluding:

> While defects in present credit control mechanism noted here, suggest that as internal program you explore possibility of expanding authority of present Bank of Japan to enable it to contribute more effectively to credit control and related elements of stabilization program.[42]

The Finance Division had hoped the new banking law would be

ready for submission to the Diet in November,[43] but with Draper's cable progress came to a halt, and planning remained paralysed in anticipation of a final opinion from Washington. Cagle was incensed by the criticisms and composed a 19-page memorandum defending his proposal and insisting that immediate reform was necessary:

> It is readily conceded that the proper timing of changes is extremely important but there is great danger in delaying action too long or until a completely satisfactory stage is set for the triumphal entrance of a new monetary authority.[44]

The ESS-FI planners realised, perhaps too late, that proposals for 'democratic' change, even if consciously designed not to retard recovery, were not to be welcomed enthusiastically by Washington. Thus, LeCount and Cagle began to emphasise the possible benefits of legal reform to the stabilisation effort:

> It is felt that delay of all proposed action until after stabilization is unrealistic since some changes in monetary and credit matters are necessary to accomplish stabilization. Necessary fundamental changes can best be accomplished only after a strong and properly constituted policy making and regulatory and supervisory body is created . . . The principal purpose of the proposed changes is to remove the influence of temporary politics and . . . to coordinate controls.[45]

In Korea in 1950, Federal Reserve experts working on new banking legislation were confronted with similar economic conditions and the same pressure for stabilisation from Washington. There, as in Japan, the American financial experts extolled the benefits of legal revision:

> . . . banking reform was only a secondary problem compared to budgetary reform . . . Nevertheless, we went ahead with our work in the belief that our recommendations, in addition to correcting many of the structural shortcomings and operational deficiencies of the banking system and providing a framework within which other reforms could be undertaken . . . would contribute to at least some degree to stemming the inflationary tide.[46]

While the Finance Division forcefully defended its proposal, Washington appears to have decided firmly against the immediate imposition of Cagle's plan. Draper's second cable, transmitted to

SCAP on 15 December 1948, confirmed this stand and strongly advised the ESS to devise an alternative programme of reform in conjunction with the stabilisation effort:

> . . . we assumed most practical approach would be interim program to expand authority of present Bank of Japan. View here is such a program would provide Bank of Japan with controls sufficiently powerful to permit it to curb credit and thus play its part in stabilization program. This would not preclude more extensive changes in monetary and central banking system if and when further study, especially of your proposed banking board, should prove such changes practicable and desirable.
>
> Interim program might be accomplished by amendment of Bank of Japan law . . . to grant such additional powers [in the] control of money and credit as may be deemed feasible.[47]

In essence, the Under Secretary recommended that the powers which Cagle had hoped to see vested in an independent Banking Board be transferred instead to the existing Bank of Japan. Draper, in line with conventional American thinking, appears to have believed that central banks instinctively work to support the value of money and promote conservative financial practices. Thus, the removal of monetary authority from the politicians and bureaucrats of the Finance Ministry and its centralisation in the Bank of Japan seemed, to Washington, a significant institutional advance in the effort to stop inflation. Draper was not totally insensitive to the arguments in favour of more extensive legislative change, and seemed indeed to support the principle of Cagle's Banking Board, but economic stabilisation was his primary concern and the only justifiable reforms (at least in the short term) were those which apparently favoured it.

The Finance Division was jolted by Washington's recommendations but appeared resigned to submitting to the higher powers. Cagle, however, as architect of the abandoned reform legislation, continued to defend his work and harshly criticised the 'interim program'. Cagle protested that the Bank of Japan already exercised many of the prerogatives which Draper sought to vest in it legally, but nevertheless had not shown any inclination to take a firm line on inflation. Questioning the assumption that a central bank would necessarily be financially responsible, Cagle warned:

> In the face of the known facts and reports as to the manner in which the Bank of Japan has exercised its policy making powers and

carried out its financial and credit operations, it would seem unnecessarily hazardous to further concentrate broad policy making powers, coupled with broad and completely discretionary control over the actual purse strings, in the Bank of Japan — even if it operated under a board of directors . . . This seems doubly dangerous to one who realizes that the Bank of Japan is largely a one-man institution, not inhibited by specific legal checks and controls.[48]

While recognising that Draper's 'proposal' was actually a directive, the Finance Division was convinced that legal reform and economic rehabilitation were not incompatible and remained committed to broader institutional change. Thus, working from Cagle's criticisms of the 'interim program', LeCount hastily devised a compromise scheme which appeared both to satisfy Washington's goals and offer some limited structural reform. The Finance Division no longer argued for a Banking Board or a new general banking law but suggested that

> . . . as a compromise toward Washington's opinions, we would be prepared to accept . . . the establishment by appropriate legislation of a Policy Control Board within the framework of the Bank of Japan. This Board would be separate and apart from the bank's board of directors. It would be the determiner and be responsible for most, if not all, of the policies and responsibilities previously contemplated for the Banking Control Board and with power to direct the Bank of Japan . . . to implement its various decisions and recommendations.[49]

The proposed Policy Board was to resemble Cagle's Banking Board closely in structure, functions and powers. LeCount recommended that the new committee have five voting members: four with private-sector expertise in finance, commerce and agriculture appointed by the Cabinet, and the Governor of the Bank, *ex officio*. Representatives from the Finance Ministry and the Economic Stabilization Board (ESB) were also to sit on the Policy Board, but without voting privileges. The new body 'would formulate important monetary, credit and other banking policies and would have power to direct execution thereof through the present directorate and operating management of the Bank of Japan'.[50] The Board was thus to be organised within the Bank's legal structure but was to be concerned solely with policymaking, the actual implementation of its decisions to proceed through the existing Bank mechanisms. The specific responsibilities to be transferred to the

Board (primarily from the Minister of Finance) were considerable and included determination of the discount rate, establishment of rates of interest for the financial institutions and regulation of market operations.[51] In sum, LeCount's plan aimed to increase the monetary control powers of the Bank of Japan, as Washington had demanded, but sought to vest the increased policymaking authority in a representative committee rather than in the Governor alone.

The Finance Division proposal was transmitted to the Army Department on 14 February 1949. A week later, while the plan was being studied in Washington, Joseph M. Dodge, the newly appointed economic advisor to SCAP (whose role is considered in detail in Chapter 5), sent Draper a personal cable from Japan on the banking reform programme. Dodge expressed his support for the centralisation of monetary controls in the Bank of Japan and endorsed the formation of a Policy Board, maintaining that the present management of the Bank was 'not competent . . . to exercise central banking authority'.[52] Draper trusted Dodge's economic counsel, having worked with him on the currency reform in Occupied Germany, and relayed official approval of the ESS–FI proposal to SCAP on 25 February. Democratisation was hardly foremost in the Under Secretary's mind, as his cable stated 'no objection here to Policy Control Board on the basis that . . . [the] Board will increase likelihood of success of economic stabilization program'.[53]

The necessary legal provisions were drafted by the Japanese authorities under Dodge's personal supervision and on 3 June 1949, the Bank of Japan Law was amended to provide for a new Policy Board. Draper and Dodge were not prepared to allow a potentially disruptive full revision of the Bank's charter,[54] so the Policy Board was simply grafted onto the existing 1942 legislation. The operational structure of the Bank and, most importantly, its legal relationship to the Ministry of Finance were thus left unaltered, with the Board merely assuming the *de jure* position of what had previously been the *de facto* role of the Governor. The new committee was granted some substantial monetary powers but, being a part of the Bank, was not guaranteed legal independence from the Finance Minister's control.[55] Significantly, key supervisory responsibilities — including the authority to examine banks, grant licenses and regulate branching — were not transferred to the new committee, but remained under the control of the Ministry of Finance. In short, the wartime 'chain of command' stretching from the bureaucracy to private-sector finance via the Bank of Japan was not broken — or even substantially weakened — by the American legislative initiative.

SCAP had great hopes for the Policy Board when it was launched in the summer of 1949, expecting it to contribute substantially to economic stabilisation and simultaneously to establish democratic principles in the determination of monetary policy. Unfortunately, the Board failed to reach the Americans' goals in either respect, emerging as a powerless and unassertive appendage to Japan's economic bureaucracy. Only a year after its foundation, Dodge lamented,

> There has been no evidence the Policy Board has proved to be effective as a control device. . . Apparently it is not a satisfactory substitute for statutory controls or for the personal administration and authority heretofore exercised by the Governor of the Bank of Japan and the Finance Minister.
>
> As far as we know, the Policy Board has taken no constructive action to strengthen the position of the Japanese banks. . .
>
> There does not appear to be close coordination of the financial policies of the Bank of Japan and Government fiscal policies.[56]

As Cagle had warned, even with increased monetary powers vested in the Policy Board, the Bank of Japan did not emerge as a force for stabilisation. Rather, as described in more depth in Chapter 5, the Bank's continued adherence to loose credit policies after the 1949 legal revision undermined Dodge's austerity plan and frustrated the re-emergence of the market mechanism. In trusting that all central banks naturally tend to promote financial stability, Draper and Dodge made that error, so common during the Occupation, of assuming that Japanese organisations would behave in the same manner as their Western counterparts.

The Policy Board proved equally disappointing to the Americans who had hoped it would democratise policymaking in the Bank of Japan. The Board fell immediately under the control of the Bank's Governor, the powerful Ichimada Hisato, later nicknamed 'the Pope'. Dodge commented in 1951 that

> There is little evidence that the Policy Board of the Bank of Japan has met its responsibility as an independent policy-establishing body and less evidence that it has provided any real banking leadership. Apparently it is completely subservient to the Governor of the Bank.[57]

Thus, despite the existence of the Board, the Bank of Japan quickly reverted to effective one-man control, a situation which has persisted through the subsequent decades. As in several other cases, notably that of the Currency Control Board, the occupiers sought to 'democratise' and promote policy independence by appointing a committee to assume the authority formerly vested in an individual. The *Oriental Economist* commented cynically:

> Many boards and committees were created in Japan during and after the war, but few of them achieved any noteworthy results. . . The major fault with committees and boards in the past was the complete lack of autonomy. Hence, their policies were made to reflect strongly the policies and attitudes of officialdom, particularly as their activities mainly consisted of swallowing original plans drafted by the Government or Ministries in their entirety or with minor revisions.[58]

Certainly, in the case of the Policy Board, SCAP's use of such a contrivance for democratisation was shown to be superficial, unsuited to Japanese conditions and ultimately futile.

Thus, in the end, the legal reform of banking had a minimal impact and was hardly satisfactory from the American viewpoint. While the amendment of the Bank of Japan Law was only conceived as an 'interim program', it was the only major legislative change which SCAP was able to accomplish in this area. There was some discussion in 1950 of an American 'banking mission' and renewed efforts at legislative revision,[59] but as the Occupation wore down, reform was increasingly circumscribed by authorities in Washington who wished to see the Japanese gradually assume a greater, more independent role in the determination of their own governmental affairs. Thus, although Draper had comfortingly assured the occupiers that the time would someday be right for the establishment of a Banking Board, institutional and legal reform of this magnitude never again appeared practicable during the Occupation. When Cagle's legislative plan was officially 'postponed' in the autumn of 1948, any possibility of the Americans effecting a broad, progressive reform of the Japanese banking system appears to have been finally lost.

In retrospect, however, it seems unlikely that Cagle's reforms would have produced results in democratisation or financial stabilisation more satisfying to the Americans than the 1949 'interim program' did. Cagle's grand plan, like the Policy Board scheme, appears to have been flawed in the assumption that the 'Americanisation' of institutions and statutes would guarantee the 'Americanisation' of policies and practices in Occupied Japan. As one expert commented on the Finance Division legislative programme:

> The proposal for a new banking law appears to be an attempt to transplant, with some variations, the Federal Reserve Act . . . from the United States to Japan without adequate consideration of the many fundamental differences which exist between the two countries and with little regard to Japanese customs and psychology. No greater error can be made than to assume that, because certain laws have been proved to be desirable and effective in the United States, they are equally desirable and may be expected to be equally effective in other countries where economic, financial, social, cultural and psychological conditions are radically different from those existing in the United States.[60]

As Welsh realised in the spring of 1948, the success of the Finance Division reforms was ultimately dependent upon the Japanese who would populate the newly formed bodies and reorganised institutions. The ESS-FI planners did not adequately address the problems inherent in their attempt to create powerful countervailing forces in a government administrative structure where a basic communality of interests and outlooks existed. Cagle, for all his legal acrobatics, could in the end only express his 'pious hope' that the proposed regulatory apparatus would prove democratic and financially responsible.[61] Legal independence, clear statutory powers and limitations, and a 'democratic' organisation could not alone guarantee Cagle's Banking Board an autonomous and significant role in the Japanese economic policymaking apparatus. The experience of the Economic Stabilization Board, an institutional experiment which proved highly disappointing to its American creators, provides a picture of what the Banking Board's development might well have resembled under Japanese stewardship. In short, creating a system which mirrored the Federal Reserve in operation and spirit, rather than simply in organisational structure, would seem to have been all but impossible given the conditions, traditions and attitudes which prevailed in Occupied Japan.

The Japanese government made an effort to revise the banking laws in 1950, but with the goal of turning the clock back rather than of completing the occupiers' legal 'Americanisation'. The Banking Bureau of the Ministry of Finance drafted extensive new legislation which aimed to confirm and strengthen the Ministry's controls over the private banking sector and restore the monetary powers recently transferred to the Policy Board. While Japanese bankers were reluctant to embrace American economic democracy, they were also ill-inclined to allow the legal sanction of a Finance Ministry hegemony. The proposal provoked a fierce reaction from the Bank of Japan, which stood to lose the most in the reform, and from the commercial banks, especially the prefectural institutions, which feared redoubled bureaucratic restrictions.[62] Although the Banking Bureau went to lengths to produce a law palatable to the Americans, Dodge and SCAP balked at the centralisation of monetary control authority and supervisory responsibilities in the Finance Ministry.[63] Ultimately, under the weight of domestic resistance and SCAP disapproval, this second major legislative reform proposal under the Occupation was publicly discredited and abandoned.

Thus, Japanese laws relating to banking and finance remained virtually unchanged over the Occupation's tenure. New legal standards of banking practice were not enacted and revisions in the regulatory structure were not realised. Despite the institution of the Policy Board, established interests in the bureaucracy had managed to retain broad powers over the central bank, the commercial institutions and the formulation of monetary policy. In short, the Americans, for all their expressions of dedication to demilitarisation and democratisation, had only effected the most superficial alterations to the wartime legal foundations of Japanese banking. Under the pressure of economic realities and the weight of existing financial arrangements, the maintenance of the *status quo* in Japanese banking once again took precedence over the pursuit of 'Americanising' reform.

5

Finance Under the Dodge Line, 1949–52

Despite Washington's success in redefining the objectives of US economic policy in Japan, American efforts to reform Japanese finance did not cease in 1949. Although many commentators have maintained that Occupation reformism was snuffed out by Stateside conservatism, in fact, the last years of SCAP's tenure saw a renewed commitment to the 'Americanisation' of Japan's banking system. This final reform initiative, pursued under the direction of Joseph Dodge, differed in basic approach from the previous efforts of the Antitrust and Finance Divisions, however. Whereas the earlier, unrealised proposals treated the financial sector as an essentially independent entity, detached from the greater structure and functions of the Japanese economy, Dodge's programme aimed at merging financial reform into overall economic policy. Thus, rather than being abandoned under the narrow 'reverse course' agenda, banking reform was reinterpreted and eventually integrated into the Occupation's final push for economic reconstruction, self-sufficiency and stabilisation.

The banking system is an essential component of any capitalist economy, with a crucial intermediary role and pervasive financial and administrative links with industry, commerce and government. Although the relationships between finance and other economic sectors vary from nation to nation, the basic interdependence guarantees that banking reform will have implications for the economy as a whole and that, in turn, general economic policy will have an effect on the operations and structure of the financial world. Thus, while SCAP planned, debated and ultimately failed to implement comprehensive banking reform, finance did not remain static, but evolved in line with the dynamic economic realities of the time. An appreciation of the economic conditions and policies of the years preceding the 'reverse course' is necessary, therefore, for a fuller understanding of financial development under the Occupation and the integrated economic and banking reforms of Joseph Dodge.

During the first three years of occupation, SCAP did not assume a consistent, active role in the formation of economic policy in Japan. As the occupiers were concerned primarily with demilitarisation and democratisation programmes, the relatively mundane task of charting economic reconstruction was delegated for the most part to the Japanese government. The Americans were prepared to take an assertive stand on certain issues with social or political implications (such as the war indemnities and the land reform) but, lacking sufficient manpower and expertise, the Occupation was in no position to assume direct control of day-to-day economic administration. SCAP contented itself with the role of regulator, monitoring the work of the authorities and applying pressure when necessary, but on the whole leaving the Japanese with significant latitude in the economic sphere.

From soon after the surrender, the Japanese government exhibited a strong inflationary bias and an overtly interventionist approach in economic policy. Believing that a deflationary collapse was near, the authorities sought to avert diaster by pumping great infusions of funds into the economy and taking direct action to support the shattered industrial sector. The government's economic position was devised largely by Ishibashi Tanzan, Finance Minister from 1946 to 1947, who prescribed expansionary financial policies to compensate for the cancellation of the indemnities and forceful governmental stimulation of the private economy to stir recovery. Ishibashi maintained that industrial production could be increased under the post-surrender conditions of unemployment and under-utilisation of capital by 'priming the pump' through inflationary fiscal and monetary policies.[1] Ishibashi would seem to have been a better politician than an economist, however, for while the government's policy was far more palatable to the populace and industry than the more economically-sound option of enforced austerity, such an inflationary programme was financially ruinous.

Thus, from 1946 to 1948, the Japanese pursued a policy which one member of the ESS later described derisively as an 'Alice in Wonderland' structure of economic 'make-believe'.[2] On the fiscal side, the government sought to promote employment and bolster the standard of living through increased public-works spending and the widespread subsidisation of commodities. Such an expansionary programme was possible only through deficit spending and, as the vast majority of the debt was assumed by the Bank of Japan, its effects were highly inflationary. Although the subsidies helped to keep consumer prices low and supported what little foreign trade Japan had at the time, these government payments had the effect of sheltering inefficient producers from market forces and directing scarce resources into economically sub-optimal uses.[3]

In financial policy, Ishibashi sought to stimulate industrial recovery by providing capital to targeted industrial sectors through government channels and selective controls over private credit. Under the 'priority production' scheme, certain key industries (such as coal and steel) were given preferential access to funds from commercial institutions and from a huge new government organ, the Reconstructon Finance Bank (RFB). Founded in 1947, the RFB was intended to be the engine of Japanese recovery, supplying vast amounts of capital — it accounted for one-quarter of all bank loans advanced in 1947-8[4] — for the rehabilitation of industry. The Bank was nominally underwritten by the government, but as the majority of its funds were supplied by the Bank of Japan, it developed into a prime engine of inflation.

SCAP was concerned with the economic effects of Japanese policy, but was more sensitive to the political and social desirability of maintaining an optimistic and superficially progressive economic environment, which Ishibashi's spendthrift policy succeeded in doing. Since many of the bureaucrats of the ESS espoused 'New Deal' thought on central planning, the Japanese were supported and encouraged in extending governmental intervention in the economy. The Americans tolerated the increasing government deficits and RFB expansion, but insisted on the enforcement of a system of rationing and price controls in an attempt to restrain inflation and ensure an equitable distribution of scarce goods.[5] The Japanese were not enthusiastic about such controls (which suggested the austerity of the war years) and only pursued the SCAP policy half-heartedly, never managing to break the wage-price spiral. However, as the Americans were preoccupied with democratising reform and lacked the personnel to supervise the government's work closely, the laxity of the Japanese authorities and the increasing economic difficulties were accepted with resignation by the policymakers of SCAP.

Ishibashi's programme did not achieve particularly impressive economic results, although the conditions it created helped maintain social and political stability during unsettled times. Under the inflationary policy, reconstruction proceeded at a brisk, though not spectacular pace. The growth was not even, however, as some industries, especially those favoured by 'priority production', recovered much faster than others. Unemployment was kept low and living standards gradually increased, yet at the cost of a potentially disastrous inflationary trend and widespread government intervention in the market-place. While Ishibashi looked with indifference upon inflation, it clearly was a tremendous problem: the consumer price index almost tripled during 1947 and nearly doubled again in the following year. An equally serious challenge to Japan's long-term economic health was presented by the pervasive official controls over the economy. As the economist Tsuru Shigeto commented in 1949:

> Prices have been so long controlled and their structure so distorted that, for example, the price of steel quoted the consumer is only one-quarter of its cost of production; the balance is made up by subsidies. Wages have lost their normal function of reflecting the relation between supply and demand of labor . . . while the exchange rate is no longer an equilibrator of international transactions. In short, the disequilibrium of the economy has been artificially maintained — indeed aggravated. Under these circumstances, the basic principle of supply and demand, which is a prerequisite for rational utilization of resources, is disregarded, and all kinds of waste are allowed to impede the conduct of the nation's economic affairs.[6]

With increased American interest in reconstruction under the 'reverse course', inflation and the distorted internal economic structure became sources of great concern to Washington. Draper and his associates were convinced that major economic change was necessary to prevent Japan from becoming permanently reliant on US financial support. The general consensus developed in Washington during 1948 that the establishment of a self-sufficient Japan hinged on the nation's ability to re-enter international markets on a competitive basis and independently generate the funds for essential raw material imports (which were then being supplied as American aid). The policymakers were well aware, however, that the desired normalisation and expansion of overseas trade, and thus long-term economic independence, were clearly unattainable as long as the existing system of multiple exchange rates, export subsidisation and strict official supervision remained in place.[7] Significantly, the Washington bureaucrats seem to have recognised that the setting of a single ¥-$ rate, the re-opening of free foreign commerce and the development of a viable export sector were only possible, in turn, through the restraint of inflation, the reduction of government economic controls and the streamlining of Japan's subsidised, inefficient industries.[8]

Proposals for the reform of Japanese economic policy emerged from both sides of the Pacific during 1948. The State Department, SCAP and the Economic Stabilization Board each offered plans designed to control inflation, but only through the use of strengthened government controls or the injection of increased US aid. These schemes were unacceptable to the conservative, thrift-minded Under Secretary of the Army, however, who advised in the official report of his 1948 mission to Japan that an austerity programme based on strict budgetary retrenchment and the promotion of exports was an economic necessity.[9]

Since the Draper group did not elaborate a detailed recovery plan, the concerned Washington agencies expeditiously dispatched a 'technical' mission to make more-specific recommendations on future SCAP economic policy. This delegation, led by Ralph Young of the Federal Reserve Board, concluded that the opening of trade should be given the highest priority and that a single exchange rate should be set by the end of 1948. The Mission's report outlined the economic policies needed to restore Japanese self-sufficiency, including a 20 per cent cut in the national budget, a more restrictive monetary policy, the progressive elimination of subsidies and the promotion of efficient, export-oriented production.[10] Both SCAP and the Japanese balked at Young's proposed austerity programme, believing it unnecessarily strict and potentially disastrous, and did not immediately alter their economic approach.[11] Washington had decided that change was imperative, however, and in December transmitted to SCAP the so-called 'Nine Points', a list of recommended economic initiatives based on the Young proposals. This cable, like many of Draper's, was more a directive than a suggestion and established stabilisation and the advancement of trade as the immediate economic objectives of the Occupation.

Both the Supreme Commander and the Washington authorities recognised the technical and political skill necessary for the successful implementation of an austerity programme, so Draper arranged for the dispatch of an expert mission to Japan charged with overseeing the enforcement of the new policy line. For its leader, Draper selected Joseph M. Dodge, his trusted colleague from the German currency reform, who was named Financial Advisor to General MacArthur with full responsibility for Occupation economic policy in Japan.[12] From his appointment in early 1949 until the Peace in 1952, Dodge reigned as a virtual 'economic czar' — or, as Ted Cohen called him, the 'Lord High Imperial Accountant'[13] — holding almost unlimited authority in the American camp. With a mandate from Washington and the full trust of MacArthur and Marquat, Dodge assumed firm personal control of the US reconstruction programme, giving SCAP its first (and only) experience of real leadership in economic and financial policy.[14]

Joseph Dodge's deeply-held economic philosophy strongly coloured his efforts in Japan. Born the son of a poster painter, Dodge (of no relation to the automotive family) was a classic American 'self-made man', rising from office messenger boy to Chairman of Detroit's largest commercial bank and President of the American Bankers' Association. From his personal experience, Dodge was thoroughly convinced of the natural superiority of the American democratic, free-enterprise system which made such 'rags-to-riches' advancement possible. Like many of his generation, Dodge was greatly affected by the Depression, and had developed a life-long mistrust of speculation and a profound faith in financial soundness and economic stability. SCAP's new Financial Advisor held to a down-to-earth, pragmatic conservatism in all matters political and economic, tending to look at issues with the cool, analytical eye of a banker. In short, Joseph Dodge presented the aspect of the archetypal Midwestern businessman — practical, capable, steadfastly American and highly suspicious of politicians, big government and anything suggestive of socialism.[15]

Dodge was appalled by the economic conditions he discovered in Japan: the profligate deficit spending, the irresponsible practices of the RFB, the extensive government involvement in the private economy and the apparent absence of any normal market mechanism. In his press statement of 7 March 1949, Dodge gave a scathing evaluation of the Japanese economy in a blunt, didactic manner:

> [Japan] cannot afford to waste any existing elements of strength supporting the unrealistic distortions and dislocations of an inflationary trend. A postponed readjustment inevitably will be extremely serious and of much longer duration.
>
> It is the height of folly to point with pride at an increasing production index or increasing exports which may actually represent only increased U.S. aid, increased subsidies and increased deficits . . . There should be general recognition that an increasing part of the national output will be needed for years ahead to replace the free goods now coming from the United States, which cannot come forever.
>
> These are the simple propositions governing economic policy. They are hard truths and not pleasant to hear but they are no more inexorable than the facts themselves.
>
> The problems cannot be met by any form of monetary miracle

or fiscal policy alone. They can be met only by increased production at less cost, sound fiscal and monetary policies, increased exports and a continued domestic self-denial.[16]

Dodge's lesson was clear: Japan had to face economic reality, live within its means and stop attempting to conjure up false prosperity and an unfounded sense of optimism.

SCAP's Financial Advisor thus called for a strict austerity programme with a co-ordinated attack on government intervention in the economy. Although Dodge's initiative has often been portrayed as little more than a narrow stabilisation effort, his objectives were actually much broader than many observers have suggested. Control of the runaway inflation was necessarily of prime concern, but Dodge realised that the achievement of price stability would not alone guarantee the smooth progress of economic recovery. In Dodge's opinion, not only did the economy have to be stabilised, but its very workings had to be improved by the restoration of the market mechanism, the promotion of industrial efficiency, the application of US aid to productive uses and the re-establishment of a sound business environment. 'Democratisation' was not a term which Dodge felt comfortable with, yet he certainly aimed to lay the foundations of an American-style 'democratic' economy — that is, a competitive, free-enterprise, decentralised, capitalist economy — as the basis for Japan's economic resurgence.[17]

In policy planning, Dodge drew heavily on the previous recommendations of the Draper and Young Missions but, in the end, the new economic initiative bore the clear impression of his own strong personal philosophy. The programme — which came to be called the 'Dodge Line' — was based on four main policy thrusts: 1. the balancing of the national budget; 2. the curtailment of RFB loans and the reform of US aid administration; 3. the reduction of government subsidies and direct economic controls; and 4. the application of a single ¥-$ exchange rate.

The cornerstone of Dodge's plan was the balanced budget requirement. Recognising that deficit spending was the prime contributor to the inflation,[18] Dodge was adamant in his calls for fiscal reform:

An effective stabilization requires relating all policy decisions to the Government budget as a primary instrument of financial policy.

It is government which turns on the spigots of inflation and government which must turn them off. Inflation must first be sterilized at the source.[19]

The Japanese defended their expansionary policies but Dodge was resolute and, with the support of Washington and SCAP, he finally managed to impose his views. The government was required to submit a balanced consolidated budget for fiscal 1949, the first such document in over a decade. Dodge demanded that all government spending be reflected in the new budget, including outlays for subsidies and public works which had previously been hidden in the debt-plagued 'Special Account'. In the end, the 1949 'Dodge budget' showed a considerable surplus — termed 'superbalanced' at the time — with revenues exceeding expenditure by over ¥250 billion, a tremendous sum considering that the 1948 cumulative deficit was only ¥62.5 billion.[20] The deflationary effect of this surplus was diffused somewhat by allocating only half for debt retirement, the remainder being used for new capital investment. Nevertheless, the fiscal retrenchment had a sobering effect on the Japanese government, which was forced to raise taxes, dismiss 140,000 employees and slash public works expenditure (described by Dodge as the 'least wisely administered and least productive' use of national funds) by a third.[21]

Dodge's second target was the Reconstruction Finance Bank. While the Financial Advisor was clearly aware of the Bank's inflationary policies, he seems to have been more concerned that the RFB had been extensively used as a political tool and thus did not adhere to sound business practices or make a valuable, economically efficient contribution to recovery. W.W. Diehl, a member of the Dodge Mission, commented:

> The history and description of current activities of the RFB reveal unsound banking policy and practice, corruption, bribery and primary political motivation. On the constructive side, there apparently is little to be said; certainly no strong case has been presented for the further expansion of this institution.[22]

Dodge fully concurred, cabling Washington after only two weeks in Japan that the RFB '. . . is a device to return to industry losses caused by cancellation of war indemnity claims on Government . . . Industry inclined to assume loans are gifts. Primarily used to avoid difficult political decisions.'[23] The Bank resisted closure tenaciously, arguing that its contribution was necessary for 'lubricating the wheel of financial operation so that it may revolve smoothly in accordance with the deflationary policy'[24] — an assertion dismissed by Dodge as 'tripe'.[25] Thus, in September 1949, after several months of progressively reduced operations, the RFB was instructed to close its doors. All of the ¥109 billion of outstanding RFB debentures was amortised in fiscal 1949, although the Bank's poor record on recovering loans meant that the majority of this sum had to be drawn from the national budget and US aid funds. As two-thirds of the bonds were held by the Bank of Japan, the mass redemption, like the 'superbalanced' budget, had a potent deflationary effect.

In conjunction with the closure of the Reconstruction Finance Bank, Dodge introduced a new government account called the US Aid Counterpart Fund which he hoped would assume the legitimate invest-ment functions of the RFB and provide for the more efficient use of American grants to Japan. Dodge was concerned that US aid had been wasted by the Japanese in the early years of the Occupation, when American supervision was lax and most of the funds were used to subsidise increased domestic consumption or inefficient industrial pro-duction. Therefore, after 1949, all transfers were collected in the new account (which was modelled on similar arrangements for Marshall aid in Europe), allowing for a precise official reckoning of US con-tributions. Under this strict new system, the occupiers were given greater control over the distribution of aid funds, which Dodge intended to target for 'the retirement of government debt and for capital investment purposes which contribute directly and quickly to economic reconstruction'.[26] Dodge saw the Counterpart Fund as a non-inflationary, 'sound and proper' substitute for irresponsible govern-ment spending and RFB activities which, under SCAP control, would never be allowed to degenerate into a 'political grab bag'.[27]

The third main thrust of the Dodge Line was the phasing out of government subsidies and price controls, with the goal of re-establishing free-market economic relationships in Japan. Dodge asserted that the existing level of government intervention caused fun-damental market distortions, promoted the misallocation of resources and upset the natural incentives for efficiency and profitability.[28] Presumably, the lifting of the artificial, largely politically-motivated controls would expose inefficient producers to competition, force industrial rationalisation and allow for the more natural determina-tion of prices, consumption, allocation and investment. Government intervention was so pervasive and so important to some sectors of the economy (particularly export industries and agriculture), however, that Dodge was unable to free the market mechanism immediately. Subsidies were, in fact, increased during the stringency of 1949, but by the early 1950s rationing was ended, prices were decontrolled and subsidies were radically slashed.[29] Government involvement in the economy was still great (especially in finance, as will be discussed later) but the most obvious, and to Dodge the most dangerous, forms of direct control were successfully removed.

Finally, Dodge sought to set a single ¥-$ exchange rate and encourage the return to more conventional arrangements in international commerce. The normalisation of overseas trade was, of course, a central concern of the American reconstruction programme, as Dodge, like Draper, believed that Japanese self-sufficiency depended upon the revival of foreign economic connections.[30] This objective was troublesome, however, for during the first years of occupation, both imported commodities and export industries had been heavily subsidised by the government, causing worries that all trade would cease when a rate was set and subsidies discontinued. Nevertheless, Dodge was determined to make Japan a competitive world producer and he hoped that the establishment of a single exchange rate and the decontrol of trade would force the streamlining of Japanese industry. Therefore, in April 1949, Dodge decreed a ¥360 to $1 rate and, in January 1950, he ordered an end to direct SCAP administration of foreign commerce, thus taking the first, crucial steps in restoring Japan's international economic autonomy.

Dodge's four-point programme focused solely on the rectification of government policy, with no provision for the direct reform or reorientation of the private-sector economy. Whereas Ishibashi and SCAP had tried to shape Japanese reconstruction through control and regulation, Dodge believed that the free market was the optimal decision-maker and that government intervention, even if directed toward constructive ends, was ultimately counter-productive.[31] The free-market system was, to Dodge, an economy's 'natural' mode of operation, which could be undermined and warped by government action, but which would eventually re-emerge when artificial restraints were removed. Thus, Dodge seems to have trusted that the proper alteration of Japanese government policy would lead to a predictable and economically favourable adjustment in the private sector — a natural correction of past distortions — making direct reform of industry and finance unnecessary. In short, under the Dodge Line, the most significant and productive economic changes were thought to be accomplished indirectly through the reduction of government intervention and the presumably inevitable resurgence of the market mechanism.

Some observers have noted with curiosity that Dodge, though a commercial banker himself, only sparingly utilised monetary policy in his fight against inflation and, in public at least, exhibited an apparent indifference to the development of Japanese finance.[32]

While the Young Mission had recommended tighter monetary controls on public and private credit sources, Dodge limited his attention to government finance, concentrating on the closure of the RFB and the creation of the Counterpart Fund. Dodge did support and oversee the establishment of the Bank of Japan Policy Board, but he did not attempt to dictate a specific monetary programme to the new administrative body once it was in place. Perhaps even more surprisingly, the Detroit bank president seemed preoccupied with the reconstruction of industry and commerce, publicly showing only marginal concern with conditions in the financial world. In his statements to the Japanese press, Dodge lambasted the government, berated industry and preached to the populace, yet remained consistently silent on the state of Japanese banking and his plans for its future.

Dodge could hardly ignore circumstances in finance, however, since many of the conditions which he bemoaned in the economy as a whole were prevalent in the banking system as well. As government prerogatives had not been fully 'demilitarised' by the occupiers, official intervention in the financial world remained extensive even four years after the surrender. Under the 'priority production' plan followed by the Japanese authorities, the autonomy of the banks and the free functioning of the market were restricted by controls over the allocation of funds, the volume of credit, the setting of interest rates and the internal practices of financial institutions.[33] The commercial banks were severely over-extended by international standards, with dangerously low capital ratios and cash margins. Loan portfolios were patently unsound, as the banks, with government encouragement, had advanced credit with little discrimination, funds often going to cover deficits and prolong the operations of non-viable firms. Japanese industry, financially crippled by the cancellation of the indemnities and spiralling inflation, had become increasingly dependent on the banks for operating funds and the supply of long-term capital. The cash-starved financial institutions had, in turn, grown dependent on the central bank for the infusions of liquid funds necessary to continue easy credit policies. In short, the financial system was riddled with the inefficient operations, unsound practices and artificial government controls which Dodge found so objectionable.[34]

Though publicly quiet, Dodge was aware of the conditions in finance, was concerned, and looked for significant change under his programme.[35] Dodge's reticence did not betray ignorance or a lack of interest in banking policy but rather a sensitivity to the financial sector's problems. Having experienced the panics of the American Depression, Dodge was understandably cautious in publicising the

101

weaknesses of the Japanese banking system.[36] As he wrote to Marquat in 1950, maintaining the people's trust in banking, or perhaps more aptly, their false sense of security, was critical at that time, for the 'dangerous situation' in finance was 'only stabilized by the ignorance of the mass of bank depositors'.[37] Although Dodge never formally elaborated a banking policy, his efforts appear to have been guided by three central objectives which reflected his 'free-market, stability-first' philosophy and complemented his overall economic plan. In essence, Dodge aimed to promote the market mechanism, increase stability and, in general terms, 'Americanise' the financial system under his broad economic programme.[38]

First, Dodge sought to reduce bureaucratic influence and involvement in the financial world. This ranged from cutting the government's role in industrial finance and decreasing direct official intervention in the internal affairs of banks, to limiting the use of selective credit controls. The goal was to strengthen the economic and administrative independence of the private institutions and to restore the market as the determiner of interest rates, savings and the allocation of funds.[39]

Second, Dodge sought to establish sound commercial banking practices in Japan. SCAP's Financial Advisor apparently considered the Japanese banks to be teetering on the brink of disaster, with insufficient capital and cash on hand for proper security, and inadequate standards in credit analysis to guarantee sound assets.[40] Safety and stability were of prime importance to Dodge, who never forgot the American 'boom and bust' of the 1920s:

> . . . banks have a primary obligation, which is the safety of the depositor's money — it is not to be freely distributed among borrowers who have more optimism than assets; banks have an obligation to the nation to maintain the strictest kind of conservatism — there can be no speculative boom unless it is financed . . . by bank loans.[41]

Third, Dodge sought to encourage the structural development of Japanese finance on the American model. With his Midwestern-banker's values, Dodge mistrusted Japanese 'mixed banking' practices,[42] deplored the existing pattern of 'indirect' finance and was appalled by the dependence of commercial institutions on the central bank occasioned by widespread 'overloan'. His ultimate goal was the establishment of a system of industrial finance in Japan like that in the United States, with a network of competitive commercial banks to supply short-term credit, active securities exchanges for providing long-term capital and well-developed money markets to facilitate the flow of funds within the economy and allow for indirect central bank control through open-market operations.[43]

While Dodge apparently had clear goals in financial policy, he did not push for a heavy-handed programme of banking reform. Dodge was loathe to force change on the private sector from above and, as a banker himself, he was particularly reluctant to dictate reform to the financial world.[44] Rather, he seems to have trusted that the changes he felt were necessary in Japanese finance would develop organically under the greater programme of stabilisation and economic normalisation. For just as Dodge believed that the free market was economically 'natural', so he appears to have held that bankers, whether in Michigan or Japan, would instinctively favour soundness, independence and, in the long run, an American-style financial system. Hence, the new, open economic environment of the Dodge Line was expected to generate a favourable reaction in finance, with bankers asserting their supposedly-innate conservative tendencies, the restored market mechanism forcing change and reform progressing without direct Occupation intervention.[45]

In what Dodge would have considered the ideal scenario, his financial objectives would have been attained with a minimum of friction or disruption, as the short, sharp shock of his four-point retrenchment programme catalysed the process of change in the banking system. The end of 'priority production' and the closure of the RFB would clear the most extensive government intervention from private-sector financing. Further artificial obstacles would presumably be removed by the new Policy Board in the Bank of Japan, which Dodge trusted would ease the government stranglehold on Japanese finance and adopt a responsible monetary policy.[46] With market forces released and the expansionary credit policies of the past curtailed, the banks would tend to scale back operations and adopt sounder loan practices. Inefficient industrial firms, meanwhile, would fail without continued subsidies, RFB support and unlimited bank credit, causing the overall demand for funds to fall. Commercial bank loans would therefore be increasingly concentrated on viable producers, thus putting Japan's limited capital to better uses and simultaneously strengthening bank assets. In the longer term, after equilibrium had been attained, active securities exchanges and money markets would develop, to the mutual benefit of industry, finance and the central authorities.[47]

In actual practice, however, the Dodge Line did not trigger the neat chain reaction in Japanese finance which its creator had expected. Events initially progressed as Dodge had hoped, as the programme was remarkably successful in controlling inflation, with consumer prices actually falling marginally over 1949 and early 1950.[48] As Dodge had anticipated, the surplus budget and the closure of the RFB caused pronounced monetary stringency in the economy. Japanese industrialists, who had complained of insufficient capital funds even under the spendthrift Ishibashi plan, became increasingly desperate under the tightened monetary conditions. The advent of austerity brought on what some authors have called a 'stabilisation panic', as business circles were thrown into a state of near-hysteria and the press was flooded with dire predictions of coming depression and imminent collapse.

Dodge welcomed these financial developments, for he believed that monetary stringency would deliver a sharp economic jolt to force industrial rationalisation and the adoption of sounder practices in banking. Dodge made no apologies for his strict deflationary policies:

> Fear is expressed that a severe shortage of funds for commercial and industrial activities will precipitate a financial crisis and force widespread business bankruptcy.
>
> The basic assumption underlying this reasoning is that credit thus far provided has been both necessary and productive. This assumption appears unwarranted. The contention that this lending should be continued involves the proof that past practice has been unquestionably sound. In fact, the record reveals that careless and large scale credit extension has encouraged speculative activity, black market transactions, rapidly rising wages and prices, ineffective management and unsound business practices.[49]

Dodge even denied there was a true shortage of funds in Japan, maintaining to Finance Minister Ikeda Hayato that there was 'a greater shortage of credit-worthy borrowers than of credit'.[50] No sympathy was shown for Japanese industry or banking as Dodge clearly hoped that the much-publicised financial problems would engender a new commitment to sound and responsible practices:

> Disinflation means that for the first time business managements have to consider the financial result of what they do, after a period during which no one had to consider these results because they were taken care of by the progress of the inflation. The more the banks have sinned against sound credit and finance in the past, the more severe are the apparent credit or liquidity crises.[51]

Nevertheless, the credit shortage did not provoke the conservative reaction in the financial world which Dodge had anticipated. Rather than contracting credit in line with Dodge's anti-inflationary policy, the commercial banks, particularly the large city banks, sharply increased their loan volume in response to the tightened monetary situation. Total advances of ordinary banks almost doubled in 1949 and jumped by a further 50 per cent in 1950 — a remarkable rate of increase considering the stability of the price level over the period.[52] The private financial institutions could not fully compensate for the curtailment of RFB and deficit spending, however, and were forced to show some increased discrimination in the allocation of credit.[53] Nevertheless, the banks were determined to stand by their customers and continued to extend loans to firms which would have been driven to bankruptcy without such support. As a result, industrial rationalisation did not progress to the extent which Dodge might have wished and the quality of bank assets was not greatly improved.[54]

The large and rapid expansion in bank credit would have been impossible without the financial and political support of the Bank of Japan. Although deposits in private financial institutions grew steadily under the Dodge Line, advances increased at a much faster pace. The 'overloan' condition thus flared, with the ratio of total loans to capital and deposits in the banking system rising from an already high 80 per cent in 1948 to 92 per cent in 1949, 102 per cent in 1950 and peaking at 108 per cent in 1951. In the city banks, which led the credit expansion, the situation was even more extreme, with the ratio topping 120 per cent in 1951.[55] The financial institutions could, of course, only maintain liquidity under these conditions by borrowing heavily from the Bank of Japan. This practice was not discouraged by the Bank's authorities, who promoted the inflationary monetary policy by giving the city banks access to virtually unlimited credit at interest below the current call market and commercial loan rates.[56]

Thus, the unsound practices in finance which Dodge found objectionable did not cease under his stabilisation policies, but may actually have intensified. As the commercial banks accelerated their extension of credit during 1949 and 1950, capital ratios declined precipitously, the quality of assets remained poor, 'overloan' worsened and dependence on the Bank of Japan for liquid funds increased. The Director of Finance in the ESS commented that

Monetary management and credit control policies in Japan during the same period in which budgetary balance has been achieved have, in my opinion, produced a situation which is potentially

> dangerous and if allowed to continue may result in economic
> disaster . . . The whole situation is patently unsound . . .[57]

The conditions in finance did not cause great concern among the
Japanese, however: the banks were enjoying record profits under the
Dodge Line[58] and many in the government, most prominently Ikeda,
pushed for even greater monetary expansion.[59] The Japanese attitude
frustrated Dodge:

> Discussing Japanese banks, [Governor] Ichimada admitted that all
> of them were in an over-loaned condition and lacked adequate
> capital . . . but he said that they were in better shape than their
> balance sheets indicated and were steadily improving their situa-
> tion. He thought that American banks placed too much importance
> upon balance sheets, wherein [Dodge] remarked how else could
> a bank be judged.[60]

SCAP's Financial Advisor appears to have found it hard to believe
that all bankers did not revere safety and soundness as much as he
himself did.

Dodge must have been particularly disappointed that the Policy
Board did not live up to his expectations. Dodge and the members
of his mission appear to have been relatively unconcerned with the
details of monetary policy, at least initially, trusting in the new
'democratic' committee to follow the Occupation's deflationary, free-
market policies.[61] As described in Chapter 4, however, the Board
turned out to be virtually impotent, and the Bank followed Governor
Ichimada's, not Dodge's, lead, pursuing an interventionist, easy
money programme. In addition to greatly increasing its advances, the
Bank supported the expansion by lowering maximum legal rates on
commercial loans,[62] temporarily transferring government deposits
from its own books to accounts in the city banks and purchasing ¥80
billion in long-term government and RFB bonds from the private sector
in 1949 and 1950.[63] To meet the needs of major firms which had
been dependent on RFB funding, the Bank stepped up its 'Accom-
modations Service' which brought together commercial banks to make
large, long-term and normally quite risky joint loans.[64] Thus,
although Dodge had managed to remove government intervention in
the economy through the RFB, the pervasive official involvement in
private finance was not simultaneously lifted. Rather, under the
expansionary credit policy, the Bank of Japan appears actually to have
extended its influence in the banking sector.[65]

Dodge had also hoped that his programme would induce change in the basic nature of Japanese capital accumulation and finance, with strong securities exchanges and money markets developing as adjuncts to the private banking system.[66] Dodge insisted on the official re-opening of the stock exchanges, which had been closed in 1945 and subsequently subjected to intense SCAP scrutiny.[67] Unfortunately, under the existing conditions, efforts to revive the securities markets and promote the system of equity financing seemed doomed to fail, at least in the short term. Incentives for increased 'direct' finance of industry seemed to be lacking, as corporations continued to rely on bank credit for investment funding. The support necessary for active stock exchanges was simply not present in Japan in 1949: the economy was volatile, very little money was available to flow into the markets, and the great prewar support of the exchanges, the *zaibatsu honsha*, had been dissolved and their divested holdings were flooding the market. Independent money markets were slow to develop as well, their growth hampered by the Bank of Japan's easy discount and loan policies and the absence of government securities (rendered unnecessary by the Dodge budget) which could have formed a solid basis for secondary bond markets.[68] In sum, under the financial conditions of 1949 and 1950, securities exchanges and money markets had little chance of significantly expanding their economic roles or developing into facsimiles of their American equivalents.

Thus, the short, sharp shock of economic stabilisation appears to have been manifestly unsuccessful in catalysing the changes in Japanese finance which Dodge considered crucial. Rather than following the Occupation's new economic programme, the financial sector seems to have reacted against it, accelerating inflationary credit policies, indulging in increasingly unsound practices and steadfastly refusing to 'Americanise' its operations. By the spring of 1950, the failure in financial policy had become obvious and Dodge grew increasingly frustrated and worried. Writing to Marquat in April, Dodge conceded that he was 'quite concerned about the banking business' and that the developments in finance appeared to be 'the principal weakness in the whole picture'.[69] The Chief of the ESS concurred, terming the situation 'alarming',[70] a sentiment echoed by American observers on both sides of the Pacific over the next several months. By mid-1950, over a year after the imposition of the Dodge Line, the occupiers finally recognised that financial policy had gone seriously wrong and that new, greatly modified reform efforts were necessary.

In November 1950, Dodge submitted to Marquat an extended

memorandum entitled 'Banking and Bank Credit' in which he presented a concise analysis of the financial situation and outlined the policies he wished to see pursued in the last years of occupation. The issue was clearly of high priority to MacArthur's Financial Advisor:

> The most serious economic and financial problems are related to the banking system, the expansion of bank credit, the expansion of private debt, the nature of this debt, and the progressively more substantial needs for capital funds and working capital funds as business activity expands.
>
> The low capital ratio of the banks to their deposits and loans, diminishing liquidity, high ratio of loans to deposits, expanding bank borrowings from the Bank of Japan, and the internal structure of the bank loan assets as it affects both banks and the debtors to the banks, are matters of serious concern.[71]

Dodge felt that Japanese practices and conditions were of the 'type which brought banking disaster in the United States in the 1920's'.[72] Continued adherence to 'mixed banking' principles was especially worrisome, as commercial bank credit was becoming increasingly 'frozen' in long-term capital loans under the current financial policies. Not only was the liquidity of the banks compromised by this practice, but the relative increase in long-term loans also reduced the availability of critical working capital funds and gave the banks greater, potentially anti-competitive leverage over borrowers. Dodge maintained that the only permanent solution to the problem of 'frozen' commercial bank credit was the creation of alternative, financially-sound sources of long-term capital funds. The revival of special long-term credit institutions was an option which Dodge did not completely rule out, but he seems to have remained convinced that equity financing was ultimately the best, most 'natural' answer:

> Under normal conditions [the 'frozen' credit situation] would be modified by an ability of private enterprise to convert this debt to equity or debenture or other formalized negotiable and marketable obligations. But Japan has no strong or well-established equity financing mechanism. What there is is feeble and poorly financed . . . Therefore, measures to encourage it should be developed.[73]

Dodge strongly criticised the monetary programmes of the central bank in his memorandum as well, stating that the financial dilemma had been exacerbated by

> . . . a policy of the Bank of Japan directed toward making the maximum amount of credit available and an expressed policy of cancelling the disinflationary fiscal policies of the government with the expansion of bank credit. There has been a lack of coordination between the Bank of Japan policy and Government fiscal policy. The latter may include outright conflict.[74]

In concluding his study of the financial situation, Dodge reiterated his anti-inflationary philosophy and revived an old analogy:

> The facts of the matter are that Japan must plan to develop its own capital resources to ensure its improvements and its progress, and do this from internal capital accumulations. That is savings and reinvestment. The tendency is to depend on the expansion of bank credit and this is supported by the record. The result is an expansion of bank credit which is inflationary in its effect. It does no good to close the spigot of inflation arising from government deficits while leaving another spigot open in terms of an excessive expansion of bank credit, particularly if the latter produces credit that tends to be frozen. The flow from this tap turns into icicles.[75]

Thus, by late 1950, Dodge appears to have developed a concern for monetary and financial policy which had been absent a year earlier. Dodge's goals had not changed, yet he realised that his passive, 'free-market' approach to financial reform would have to be altered. Japanese finance, he learned from experience, could not be expected to follow fiscal policy, to tend toward practices considered conventional in the West or to evolve naturally toward the American model.

Although Dodge believed that financial reform was economically imperative and that SCAP should assume a more assertive role in monetary and banking policy, he remained averse to heavy-handedly imposing change on the Japanese. At any rate, the time had passed for grand American reform schemes, as by 1950 Washington supported a scaling-back of Occupation operations and the gradual return of economic and political autonomy to the Japanese authorities. Dodge remained a powerful figure in Japan but his influence was effectively limited to fine-tuning official policy, and he could not (and would not) dictate vast changes in government or the private sector. Under the circumstances, Dodge could only work indirectly and attempt, using his authority and the leverage of his position, to discourage the practices and policies at the root of the financial problems and to exhort the Japanese to undertake meaningful change.

During the spring of 1950, SCAP and Dodge began pressing the Bank of Japan to relent in its expansionary monetary policies and give more attention to the soundness of the banking system.[76] Governor Ichimada was initially responsive and began to curb advances to the city banks on 8 May. Less than two months later, however, the Korean War erupted, and with the resulting flood of US procurement orders in Japan, the Bank decided to turn on the monetary spigot once again.[77] Dodge could only repeat his entreaties for restraint and soundness:

> I am further concerned that if in view of these conditions a continued expansion of bank credit should take place of the character that has taken place in the last two years and particularly the last six months, it will contribute to that difficulty and I am asking Mr. Ichimada as I will ask Mr. Ikeda to take these problems seriously, to study them and to assist us and we will assist them in working out proper approaches to them.[78]

Dodge repeatedly advised the Governor to reduce advances to the city banks, to work to 'unfreeze' commercial credit and to attempt to co-ordinate monetary with fiscal policy.[79] Nevertheless, Ichimada was not inclined to defer to the Americans and continued to support credit expansion and solidify the Bank's power during the Korean War boom. In the end, Dodge's exhortations apparently had little effect on the Bank of Japan's monetary programmes.

SCAP appears to have been equally unsuccessful in its independent effort to 'educate' Japanese bankers and government officials in sound, efficient and 'democratic' financial practices. Commercial bankers received SCAP tutelage on 'sound management policies' in accounting and administration,[80] while government employees from the Finance Ministry and the Bank of Japan were lectured on 'modern bank examination' and 'democratic banking law'. As the ESS reported:

> In general the objective of this program is to change, if possible, the Japanese concept that a bank is an instrument of economic penetration, to the more time-honored concept that a bank's first responsibility and function is to protect the depositor's funds through sound intelligent lending and investing policies.[81]

The educational efforts would not appear to have had a significant effect on financial practice or monetary policy, however, at least in the short term. No sudden transformation in the banking sector was apparent and SCAP could only boast lamely that 'as an illustration of the effectiveness of the [educational programme], two branch bank managers have been relieved of their duties because of incompetency'.[82]

As exhortation had apparently failed, SCAP and Dodge looked to legal reform as a potential long-term solution to the financial dilemma. While the earlier ESS-FI effort had been 'postponed' by Washington in the interest of the stabilisation programme, by 1950 the Americans were again discussing possible revisions in the legal foundations of the Japanese banking system. Marquat, increasingly frustrated with the attitudes of bankers and bureaucrats, was convinced that immediate legislative reform was necessary and he considered requesting an expert mission from the US to advise the Japanese on banking law.[83] Dodge fully agreed, stating that 'the time has come to move' on legal reform, and suggested that the revised codes should

> . . . assure greater coordination of Central Bank policy with the overall fiscal policy, provide checks against undesirable and un-warranted expansions of private bank credit . . . and limit the amount of loans made by banks to single borrowers.[84]

No advisory mission was dispatched, as Washington proved reluctant to support any reform initiatives which might alienate the soon-to-be-independent Japanese. The Banking Bureau of the Finance Ministry did oblige the occupiers by voluntarily undertaking work on a new general banking law but, as discussed in Chapter 4, the resulting proposal was predictably 'un-American' in intent and detail. The draft was entirely unacceptable to Dodge, who campaigned against it in official circles and who must have been relieved when the proposed revisions were abandoned under a storm of domestic protest.[85] Thus, although Dodge had eventually come to appreciate the possible contribution of legal reform in banking, the time was too late for the Occupation to take the lead in such a major project. By 1950, the Americans could only react to Japanese schemes for legal change and hope that no counter-productive reform proposals would be realised.

One Japanese initiative which Dodge did support was the foundation of the Japan Development Bank (JDB) in 1951. This new government institution was first proposed by the Finance Ministry in the autumn of 1950 and was regarded by the Japanese as filling the void left in long-term capital financing of basic industry by the closure of the RFB. Although Dodge was philosophically opposed to governmental banks — fearing that they could easily be exploited for political ends[86] — he was amenable to the establishment of a development bank, although for different reasons than his Japanese colleagues.[87] While Ikeda, main proponent of the JDB, wanted the bank to act as a pipeline of funds for targeted sectors,[88] Dodge felt that the new institution should be used apolitically to strengthen the banking system by refinancing 'frozen' loans. As Dodge stated:

> The primary purpose of the JDB [should be] to liquify the loan portfolios of the commercial banks and place them in a position to meet credit demands for working capital purposes now severely restricted because of the large investment in capital type loans for which there is no quick turnover.[89]

Dodge was particularly concerned about the manner in which the Development Bank was to raise its funds, as he was determined to prevent it from becoming a drain on the private sector or an engine of inflation. The Financial Advisor insisted that the Bank not issue debentures — and thus not compete with commercial institutions for funds — but that instead the necessary capital be supplied entirely from 'non-inflationary' budget appropriation and Counterpart Fund grants. The Japanese did not share Dodge's views on the JDB but they accepted his conditions, secure in the knowledge that the Occupation's term was soon to end.[90]

Perhaps inevitably, the Japan Development Bank did not prove a great success from Dodge's point of view. As the Japanese government had planned, the Bank immediately assumed an active role in direct, long-term industrial funding, while the refinancing of commercial bank loans was almost totally ignored, accounting for only 15 per cent of the JDB budget in 1952, before being totally discontinued in 1953.[91] While the Bank did not become 'politicised' like the RFB, it was closely tied to the Japanese bureaucracy from its inception and has since tended to reflect official policy in its operations.[92] Less than three months after the Peace, the government amended the JDB's charter, neatly wiping away the conditions which Dodge had imposed. The Bank was given the authority to issue debentures, borrow from the postal savings system and extend credit without the loan ceilings imposed by SCAP.[93] In short, the JDB did not assume the limited, conservative role which Dodge had designed for it, but expanded and developed along the path which the Japanese government had wished. Rather than becoming a support of the commercial banking system, the new institution evolved into a replacement for the defunct RFB and the Counterpart Fund in the marshalling of long-term credit. Hence Dodge's last and most assertive effort at strengthening finance was frustrated by the tenacity and economic single-mindedness of the Japanese.

Thus, Dodge's 'second wind' in financial policy seems to have ended as disappointingly as his first efforts. Although Dodge realised in 1950 that change in banking and monetary policy was necessary, he was ultimately unable to transform finance through exhortation, the promotion of legal reform or the creation of new institutions. Japanese banking was stronger in 1952 than in 1950 primarily due to improvements in the economy as a whole during the Korean War, and not to any of Dodge's efforts at indirect reform. None of the fundamental problems which SCAP's Financial Advisor had identified — 'overloan', unsound banking practices and assets, 'frozen' loans, an inflationary bias in monetary policy — had been beaten in the last two years of occupation.

As the American tenure in Japan came to a close, the occupiers were uniformly pessimistic about the future of Japanese finance. W.W. Diehl of the Dodge Mission, like many interested observers, stressed Japan's fundamental economic problems:

> Working almost wholly in the field of banking and finance, I am perhaps unduly conscious of the weaknesses of the Japanese banking structure and of the powerful and destructive inflationary forces at work here.[94]

E.M. Reed of ESS-FI seemed to paint an even grimmer picture:

> I am concerned with the future of Japan because of the serious lack of a politically stable group capable of carrying through with a sound financial program . . . As usual, every specific action flies directly in the face of the recognized solutions and appears to be dictated by an immediate political expedience rather than by the long-run good of the country.[95]

Dodge was equally gloomy about the long-term prospects for finance. In his final public statement in Japan he concluded sombrely that the nation was 'suffering from a plague of false legends' and 'dangerous delusions' which included the belief that

113

. . . granting progressively larger amounts of commercial bank credit for capital purposes can be substituted for the normal processes of capital accumulation, without creating current credit shortages and the possibility of later difficulties.[96]

Thus, as Dodge prepared to return to Detroit, he finally revealed his misgivings about the conditions in banking and, in so doing, publicly acknowledged his failure to establish Western practices, standards and ideals in Japanese finance.

In retrospect, Dodge was successful in reforming Japanese fiscal policy, establishing a solid exchange rate, re-opening foreign trade and, to some unclear extent, in streamlining Japanese industry with his free-market policies. Finance remained the weakest link in the chain, however, as market distortions, unsound practices and inflationary forces seemed to be squeezed from other parts of the economy into the financial sector under the Dodge Line. These results were perhaps not surprising, as financial reform, even after the 'reawakening' of 1950, was considered to be of secondary priority by Dodge and his advisors. The control of inflation and the reduction of government intervention in the private economy were the overriding economic concerns and financial policy, although clearly of importance to Dodge, was always devised and implemented in the shadow of these greater goals.

Some writers have asserted that Dodge was 'soft' on Japanese finance because he was a banker himself and that he supported the expansionary monetary policy as a 'safety valve' for deflationary pressures within the economy.[97] Little evidence exists to support such a view, however, as Dodge appears to have expressed no particular sympathy for Japanese bankers nor any interest in relieving the contractionary effects of his austerity programme. Certainly, the Financial Advisor did not recommend direct reform of banking, but this was not exceptional, as he disapproved of imposing change on any sector of Japan's private economy. Dodge was clearly sensitive to problems in finance, but it is difficult to believe he condoned the situation in banking or was anything less than disappointed and frustrated with the course of financial development. In other words, the deficiencies in Dodge's financial programme cannot be dismissively viewed as the result of a conscious decision to ignore reform in banking and monetary policy.

Dodge's greatest miscalculation in financial policy would appear to have been his trust that Japanese bankers and government officials would be guided by the same standards and priorities as their American counterparts. Dodge apparently expected that under the weight of economic realities and his incessant exhortation, the Japanese would suddenly, 'naturally' recognise the folly of their ways and economically repent. The importance of soundness, stability and the free market was so crystal clear to Dodge that he seems to have been unable to understand that the Japanese were working from a far different, though just as deeply-seated, set of economic assumptions. SCAP's Financial Advisor pictured himself as the great teacher, speaking with the voice of reason, and Japanese bankers and officials as his economically ignorant, temporarily misguided charges. In the sphere of financial policy, however, the Japanese were not inclined to learn from their conservative American mentor.

Although the Japanese found little common ground with Dodge in economic outlook, the failure of Occupation financial policy from 1949 to 1952 cannot be ascribed entirely (or even primarily) to Japanese opposition and intractability. The Japanese did not so much sabotage the American efforts as merely pursue their own financial affairs within the vast gaps in American policy. Dodge did not initially take a firm line on banking or monetary matters — certainly nothing like the dictatorial stand he assumed in fiscal planning — leaving the financial sector to adjust freely (and Dodge hoped predictably) to the changes in economic conditions. By rejecting direct reform in finance and trusting in 'natural' reactions, 'responsible' behaviour by the central bank and the 'inescapable' forces of the free market, however, Dodge seems to have forfeited any opportunity for introducing concrete, immediate change and granted the Japanese the freedom to chart their own financial development. By the time Dodge recognised the failure of his initial approach to banking reform and monetary matters, American authority in Japan was on the wane and SCAP's 'economic czar' was reduced to virtual impotence in financial policymaking.

In the final analysis, Dodge appears to have been unrealistic in his expectations and overly ambitious in his financial objectives. Like uncounted other Occupation planners, he sought to accomplish too much in too short a time and with an inadequate appreciation of Japanese conditions. One Japanese banker advised Dodge that economic difficulties were inevitable, progress was sure to be slow, and ultimate failure not unlikely under his economic programme, as he had introduced 'the self help or free economy idea' to Japan for 'the first time in history'.[98] Indeed, the transformation which Dodge envisaged in Japanese finance could almost be termed revolutionary, for he sought fundamental change — 'Americanisation' — in the very nature of the Japanese system of economic organisation and the attitudes which underlay it. Thus, Dodge — the arch-reactionary, the narrow technician, the 'Imperial Accountant' — appears in retrospect to have been as committed (and ultimately, as frustrated) a crusader for banking reform as either Welsh or Cagle, his two predecessors in the pursuit of financial democratisation in Occupied Japan.

6

Conclusions

As many commentators on the Occupation have noted, banking reform was strikingly absent from the Americans' seemingly comprehensive programme of directed change in Japan. The financial system was largely unscathed by SCAP's 'revolution from above' as the occupiers, for all their reform proposals and policy initiatives, were unable to replace old structures with new or establish 'economic democracy' and the 'American way' as the bases for future development. The Americans could boast few significant, lasting accomplishments in the reform of finance, and the Occupation's propaganda machine, which invariably inflated even the slightest SCAP successes into resounding US triumphs, remained tellingly silent on progress in banking policy. Indeed, the financial system seems in retrospect to have stood in the eye of the American hurricane of change in Occupied Japan, surrounded by a transforming storm, yet surprisingly — and apparently incongruously — spared the force of the reformist winds about it.

Most Western research on the Occupation has tended to ascribe American frustrations in institutional reform either to concentrated Japanese opposition or to the reorientation of official policy under the 'reverse course'. Writers such as Hadley and Calder have clearly stressed the importance of these factors in determining the results of US reform efforts in finance. Certainly the record shows that the Japanese did work at times to subvert American policy — as in the cases of the Industrial Bank and the JDB — and that the 'reverse course' decision-makers did press for a rapid conclusion to the 'bank question' and a compromise solution in legal revision. Nevertheless, in light of the complex and dynamic American experience in banking policy which this study has documented, indigenous resistance and Washington's conservatism hardly seem sufficient explanations for the failure of financial reform in Occupied Japan.

As a close historical analysis reveals, the US banking initiatives were consistently crippled by their planners' philosophical inflexibility and frequently enmired in the workings of the Occupation's bureaucratic machinery. In general, the Americans' grand reform proposals were inherently weak and superficial, founded on questionable assumptions and characterised by an essentially ethnocentric orientation. Conflict and confusion in the planning process and during the course of implementation put a further drag on the progress of directed change. This study suggests that these factors — deficient planning, bureaucratic factionalism and muddled administration — were more fundamental hindrances to the achievement of financial reform than Japanese resistance and the advent of the 'reverse course'. In sum, the Occupation banking programme appears not to have been thwarted by external pressures so much as paralysed by internal conditions.

Through most of their tenure in Japan, the occupiers worked without the benefit of a clearly-defined and consistent agenda in economic policy. Though all could embrace the general aim of creating a 'peaceful, democratic and self-supporting Japan', there was no consensus in the American camp on the role of economic and financial policy in the pursuit of this final goal. MacArthur's headquarters and the various concerned agencies in Washington, divided and distracted by 'crisis management', were unable to agree upon and establish a comprehensive, forward-looking framework for Occupation economic efforts. As the ambiguities of SCAP's mission were thus left unsettled, tensions predictably developed within the American policymaking structures, the most significant and well-documented being that between the desire to reform economic institutions and the pressure to maintain stability. With the occupiers' many divergent viewpoints and a lack of clear overall guidance, the uncertainties and unresolved priorities of US economic policy were inevitably manifested in bureaucratic conflict.

In banking policy, at least, internal division, debate and disorder exerted a powerful immobilising influence on American reform programmes. Under the conditions of bureaucratic 'feudalism' which existed in the ESS, inter-agency differences of opinion over means and ends were often magnified into insurmountable obstacles to progress. The confused hierarchy of Occupation command, with its numerous centres of decision-making and sources of planning, was not able to deal quickly or surely with administrative disputes, a condition which led to official indecision, drift, increased polarisation and the prolongation of friction. Certainly, as the experience of the 'bank question' demonstrates, disagreements within the SCAP bureaucracy could confuse, stall and ultimately derail proposals for change in finance. Compromise was apparently possible in some situations — as with the decision for a Policy Board — yet such hybrid solutions seemed destined to satisfy neither side in an administrative debate. In the final result, the paralysis of financial reform engendered by internal factionalism and indecision led by default to the preservation of the existing structures, practices and conditions in Japanese banking.

The 'reverse course' has often been presented as something of a *deus ex machina* which put an end to the disorder in SCAP economic policymaking and imposed a strict, pro-recovery agenda on the Occupation's efforts. Yet this conventional view is by no means confirmed by the evidence of the banking programmes, which suggests that the consequences of the 'reverse course' and the coming of Dodge were less dramatic and uniform than is commonly supposed. In neither abstract nor concrete terms, for example, can 1945–8 be seen as a period of primarily 'reform' orientation or 1948–52 as an interval of 'reconstruction' emphasis in American financial policy. If anything, the accepted notion of the 'reverse course' divide seems to be blurred and upended in the case of banking policy, as the earlier years of occupation were dominated by ESS-FI's economically responsible stance while the later stages, under Dodge's leadership, were marked by a comparatively high concern for financial change. In short, since pressures for 'reform' and 'reconstruction' were in continuous, dynamic interaction in US financial policy throughout the Occupation, the banking programmes do not lend themselves to a neat periodisation pivoted on the 'reverse course'.

One significant continuity through the Occupation was the consistent relegation of banking reform to a position of secondary importance in the American economic mission. Washington and the upper echelons of SCAP generally showed little interest in any aspects of banking policy which did not relate directly to greater efforts of socio-economic reform, inflation control or industrial recovery. Banking was clearly seen in a supporting role by most important policymakers and, at least before the arrival of Dodge, financial programmes were not discussed widely outside the concerned divisions of the ESS. Even Dodge, who believed banking reform was essential, only gave serious attention to financial affairs in the last stages of his work in Japan. Whereas in Occupied Germany, financial reorganisation was accorded a high priority — largely as a result of Morgenthau's planning and French persistence — in Japan, where finance was not considered a matter of immediate concern and there were no powerful external advocates for change, American banking reform was never pushed forward with comparable vigour or resolution.

Despite the Occupation's unimpressive record in banking reform the Americans, and the officials of ESS-FI in particular, could claim significant accomplishments in the 'readjustment' of the Japanese financial system to peacetime conditions. SCAP's achievements in this area of banking policy derived largely, it seems, from the special attitudes and conditions which underlay the work of postwar financial rehabilitation. In 'demilitarisation', ESS-FI was operating within its accepted 'private empire', and thus was able to pursue its programmes without being hindered by bureaucratic opposition or intervention. In addition, while the Japanese authorities did not see eye-to-eye with SCAP on every aspect of 'readjustment', they recognised the importance of resolving problems such as the future of trust banking, and consequently were willing to work co-operatively with ESS-FI on possible solutions. The Finance Division's rehabilitation programmes, unchallenged within the American bureaucracy and supported in principle by the Japanese, thus proceeded more smoothly and achieved more concrete, lasting results than any other US financial initiative.

As the Occupation experience in 'financial demilitarisation' exhibits, American-directed change was possible if a basic consensus on goals and methods prevailed among the involved parties. Agreement between SCAP and the Japanese government was essential to progress in the planning and implementation of reform policy, as the occupiers' directive powers in the economic sphere were limited. As noted earlier, harmony inside the US camp was an equally crucial and elusive factor, since American initiatives could easily be debilitated by inter-divisional or trans-Pacific debates over priorities and approaches. Even when Dodge imposed a unified economic plan on the Occupation bureaucracy, however, the success of financial reform was not assured, as the fundamental support of the Japanese was lacking. Change was apparently difficult enough to achieve in Occupied Japan with the benefit of a general consensus, and all but impossible without it.

Although the occupiers' debates over financial policy may have suggested otherwise, the American proposals for reform shared a common vision of an 'ideal' new Japanese banking system. In essence, the Antitrust Division, ESS-FI and Dodge all sought an 'Americanisation' of the Japanese financial sector. Exact duplication of American conditions and structures was not the precise objective, however, for the reform initiatives each aimed to introduce an idealised or 'improved' US model into Japan. Hence, Welsh proposed a banking structure even less concentrated than the American, Cagle offered a 'perfected' version of the Federal Reserve and Dodge preached a standard of financial conservatism never achieved in the United States. In sum, the proposals differed not so much in basic orientation as in method and approach. While the deconcentration plan was heavy-handed and economically impracticable, Dodge's programme indirect to the point of passivity and the scheme for legal revision fell somewhere between the two, the overall goal of 'Americanising' the Japanese banking system was fundamental.

Considering the emphasis traditionally placed on the 'reverse course' cleavage, the extent of the similarities in the ideals and outlooks of the American financial reformers may appear somewhat surprising. Nevertheless, the occupiers — from Welsh to Marquat to the Financial Advisor — were all the products of one era and one culture, and their intentions and efforts in Japan clearly reflected this common heritage. While agreement on specific policies was never assured, the reformers shared fundamental, typically-American views of economic relations, perhaps most obviously a dedication to competitive, free-enterprise capitalism and a mistrust of centralised, concentrated authority.[1] The superficial similarities of Welsh's antitrust plan, the ESS-FI legal proposals and Dodge's integrated fiancial programme may have been minimal, yet these three schemes rested on virtually identical foundations of basic principles, traditions and conventions. An analysis of the Occupation's work in banking reform would thus appear to confirm Robert Ward's conclusion that, reflecting 'the degree of ideological consensus that characterised American society in general at that time . . . the gap that separated the "New Dealers" from the "conservatives" at General MacArthur's headquarters was in many respects not that wide'.[2]

Significantly, the common viewpoint of the Occupation's financial reformers was essentially limited, inflexible and intolerant. There seems no doubt that the Americans, from Welsh to Dodge, were thoroughly convinced of the inherent superiority of US banking arrangements over those of any other nation, most particularly Japan's. Just as MacArthur held that every human has an inborn thirst for democracy, so the occupiers appear to have believed that every financial system is naturally meant to be 'American'. The US model, or rather a somewhat idealised form of it, was taken without hesitation as the absolute standard for efficiency, stability and 'economic democracy'. With the exception of some ESS-FI officials, the Americans did not seem to question the assumption that the financial structures and methods which had performed admirably in the stable, capital-rich United States would prove equally beneficial in the impoverished and confused circumstances of Occupied Japan. Unfamiliar with (and doubtless mistrustful of) foreign banking systems, the Occupation planners never considered adopting European models for the reform of Japanese banking or even contemplated such an 'un-American' practice as the nationalisation of commercial institutions. To the end, the US financial reformers self-righteously maintained that the 'American way' was a suitable and eminently desirable basis for the postwar remodelling of Japanese banking.

In finance, as in many areas of policy, the occupiers made little effort to understand Japanese views or fully appreciate local conditions. Although the officials of ESS-FI were relatively sensitive to Japanese feelings on banking reform, the Americans were inclined in general to ascribe differences of opinion between occupier and occupied to Japanese ignorance or treachery. Dodge, for example, was particularly rigid and his frequent 'conversations' with government leaders invariably degenerated into homespun homilies on financial conservatism or stern lectures on economic responsibility. Ted Cohen concluded that 'visiting experts in principle came to Japan as teachers, not students . . . They had no room in their mental baggage for the psychology and attitudes of the people for whom they had been called upon to prescribe [economic reform].'[3] Outside advisors were certainly not the only Americans wearing intellectual blinders: all the occupiers, to some extent, seemed to feel that the more the Japanese resisted a proposed reform, the more meaningful and justifiable such change became. In short, the majority of US planners held to a Manichaean, moralistic view, recognising the existence of a unique banking tradition and distinctive 'attitudes' in Japan, yet rejecting the established 'Japanese way' as inherently flawed, untenable and not deserving of serious consideration.

As the legal reform scheme and the Dodge programme demonstrate, the Americans and Japanese had far different standards of financial stability and notions of what constituted safe operations in banking. While the occupiers were appalled by Japanese practices, wary of the extent of government intervention and constantly in fear of a financial collapse, the Japanese themselves, from central bank officials to small depositors, remained remarkably sanguine. To the Americans, real stability was based on balance-sheet solidity, sound regulatory standards and the financial independence of individual institutions. To the Japanese, however, stability had historically been founded on interdependence and, in particular, on the various guarantees and direct lines of support which the government extended to the financial system. Thus, although the Americans considered official influence a manipulative, distorting force in banking, the Japanese assumed that co-ordinated central intervention, rather than statistical balance or rigorous codes of practice, was the linchpin of financial stability. In light of this fundamental difference in attitude, it seems hardly surprising that the Japanese turned a deaf ear to Dodge's sermons on 'responsible' banking.

In essence, the occupiers and the Japanese had remarkably different conceptions of economic life and divergent opinions on the optimal structure, functions and wider significance of banking. The Americans' reformist thought was based on the premiss that 'economic democracy' was universally desirable and applicable. But while the occupiers had faith in the benefits of free competition, the market mechanism and equity finance, the Japanese found the very concept of 'economic democracy' unfamiliar, unproven and in many aspects antithetical to their traditional practices, standards and perceptions. For although defeat had discredited Japan's military leaders, it had not driven the Japanese to question their basic modes of economic behaviour or their attitudes toward the form and role of the banking system. At the end of the war, the Japanese felt little enmity toward the existing financial structure, no instinctive revulsion at 'overloan' or *zaibatsu* dominance and, in sum, no imperative to reform arrangements which had served the nation so admirably since 1927. Generally satisfied, sceptical of the benefits of 'economic democracy' and not inclined to abandon the familiar in a time of crisis, the Japanese were quite understandably reluctant to embrace the occupiers' American ideals in banking.

In the final analysis, the US reform proposals in finance seem only to have promised superficial institutional changes based on an ethnocentric vision of an 'Americanised' Japan. This was, however, characteristic of the entire Occupation 'mission', which worked, in large part, to introduce the superstructures of US 'democratic' life with little regard for Japanese attitudes, circumstances or economic needs. In some cases, notably constitutional and land reform, the Occupation's confident style and unashamedly American predisposition were the forces behind impressive, lasting change in Japan. Yet the weaknesses of this approach, which have been described in terms of American idealism, optimism, ambition or, as by Yoshida, 'happy ignorance', were obvious in the failure of the banking reform programmes. The occupiers were hidebound by their fundamental assumptions that 'different' meant 'wrong', that American financial arrangements were inherently superior and that institutional change could transform basic modes of behaviour and underlying philosophical orientations. Thus, the Americans concentrated on devising schemes to implant US structures, standards and practices in Japan, rather than striving to create real incentives for long-term change or seriously addressing the fundamental differences between American and Japanese perspectives. Bagehot wrote that, 'A system of credit which has slowly grown up as years went on, which has suited itself to the course of business, which has forced itself on the habits of men, will not be altered because theorists disapprove of it'.[4] As the experience in Occupied Japan clearly demonstrated, the disapproval of a conquering army cannot be expected to ensure financial change either.

The failures of Occupation banking policy were, of course, highly significant to the reconstruction and long-term development of Japanese finance. The collapse of deconcentration, the dilution of legal reform and the passivity of Dodge's programme ensured that the *status quo* in the banking system was not directly disrupted, with basic continuities in financial relationships and personnel preserved across the defeat into the postwar period. The Occupation forfeited the role of leadership in financial development to the Japanese government, which maintained and strengthened its directive powers and interventionist attitude during the American tenure. Even in the programme of 'financial demilitarisation' the occupiers did not force a clear break from wartime conditions, only managing to accomplish the stabilisation and peacetime readjustment of the existing system. In sum, the Occupation presided over the rehabilitation of Japan's wartime financial arrangements, never directly challenging the government controls, legal contrivances or tendencies in corporate finance and structural evolution which derived from the years of militarism. As Sakakibara and Noguchi noted, 'if [the Occupation forces] had any impact on the wartime Japanese economic system, that impact concerned internal arrangements within the system and not the existence of the system itself'.[5]

The financial continuities from wartime, and in particular the maintenance of pervasive official influence in private banking, have been considered by many to be among the most important foundation stones of Japan's 'economic miracle'. Without the web of controls inherited from the war economy, preserved and fortified under the Occupation, the Japanese bureaucracy would have lacked the leverage necessary to support the 'artificially-low interest rate' policy, uphold Japan's 'closed' financial system or preferentially allocate funding to targeted industries. Had the occupiers managed to break permanently the chain of government-banking-industry ties with legal or structural reform, the ordered financial skeleton which was of such importance in co-ordinating and regulating Japan's postwar development would have been shattered. Furthermore, had the American plans for deconcentration gone forward, the commercial banks' ability to compete on an international scale and supply the sums of credit required for heavy industrialisation would surely have been impaired. While it can hardly be concluded that the success of American financial reforms would have doomed the 'miracle', the failure of the Occupation's efforts certainly allowed for the undisrupted evolution of the banking arrangements which proved crucial to the Japanese model of rapid economic growth.

Although the financial system was a central component of Japan's postwar development, it has been strongly criticised on both sides of the Pacific for being 'undemocratic' and economically inefficient. With free competition and the operations of the market mechanism frustrated by government controls and structural characteristics, critics charge that credit has been allocated inequitably and imperfectly in economic terms, leading ultimately to the perpetuation of the divisive 'dual structure'. The post-Occupation emergence of *keiretsu*, loosely organised groupings of industrial firms around major banks, has suggested a revival of the *zaibatsu* system and fuelled assertions that preferential access to credit has been used to stifle competition. The continued primacy of 'indirect finance', as supported by the government, has kept the investment options of savers limited and forced industry to remain dependent on the banking system for the bulk of external funding. In sum, many of the presumed shortcomings of the Japanese financial system which the Occupation sought, yet failed, to correct have remained unresolved and, at least to some observers, very serious economic problems throughout the postwar period.

Nevertheless, the Japanese banking system has not proven as 'undemocratic', fragile or ineffective as some of the unsuccessful American reformers might have feared. As the course of Japan's postwar development exhibits, extensive bureaucratic intervention and a concentrated commercial banking structure did not lead inevitably to the abuse of power and a compromise of democracy. Likewise, Japan's non-American arrangements in finance have not been shown to be chronically unstable or inconducive to growth. Competition between banks has been vigorous and, despite the existence of *keiretsu* groupings, the rigid *zaibatsu* organisations of the prewar years have not been resurrected. The financial sector has perhaps not proven especially dynamic or innovative by contemporary Western standards, yet neither has it stagnated under the weight of government influence, 'flawed' practices or complacent oligopoly.[6] Thus, while the development of the Japanese banking system has not been entirely ideal from an American vantage point, the postwar experience does appear to have belied the Occupation's fundamental assumption that only 'Americanised' financial arrangements could prove economically viable and supportive of a democratic society in Japan.

During the period of rapid growth, the benefits of swift economic progress seem to have more than compensated for any of the adverse social or financial side-effects of Japan's banking system. By the 1970s, however, with domestic and international conditions changing, the Japanese were forced to re-evaluate the structure, functions and operations of their financial sector. The arrangements which had served so effectively in the years of the 'miracle' were confronted with increasing social welfare demands, pressures for internationalisation, a trend toward market orientation and the economic consequences of slower growth. With the worldwide 'financial revolution' of the 1980s, change has become imperative and the transformation of Japanese banking is almost certain.[7] Although today's reformers are motivated by practical considerations of international integration and financial progress, not 'democratisation', the unattained objectives of Occupation policy — the opening of competition, the relaxation of bureaucratic strictures and the diversification of finance — may at last be embraced as practicable, desirable and indeed necessary for the future of banking in Japan.

Appendix I Measures of Banking Concentration in Japan, 1901–52

	Number of banks[a]	Paid-up capital		Loans		Deposits		
		Total ¥ million	Share of 5 largest banks (%)	Total ¥ million	Share of 5 largest banks (%)	Total ¥ million	Share of 5 largest banks (%)	Share of 11 largest banks (%)
1901	2,358	252	5.6	635	12.0	450	20.7	
1905	2,229	253	5.9	796	15.7	693	21.9	
1910	2,144	315	11.7	1,250	17.2	1,180	21.5	
1915	2,149	358	14.8	1,729	20.5	1,700	23.9	
1920	2,036	964	18.5	5,703	20.9	5,827	26.9	
1925	1,701	1,501	18.9	8,843	18.4	8,727	24.1	
1930	895	1,297	24.9	6,815	29.5	8,737	36.5	
1935	569	1,134	28.5	5,933	38.7	9,950	42.5	
1940	369	980	33.0	11,349	57.1	24,670	41.8	
1946[b]	69	2,031		138,671		144,868		46.4
1947[b]	69	2,119		161,476		234,375		51.8
1948	75	14,729		324,066		505,349		52.1
1949	74	16,170		522,304		792,018		59.4
1950	76	19,131		704,726		1,048,564		59.1
1951	80	25,763		994,738		1,506,308		56.8
1952	85	29,545		1,258,660		2,223,820		56.7

Notes: a. Includes 'ordinary' banks, savings banks and government financial institutions.
        b. Total of 'old' and 'new' accounts.

Sources: Number of banks from Bank of Japan, Statistics Department, *Hundred year statistics of the Japanese economy*, Bank of Japan, Tokyo, (1966), pp. 194–5. 1901–40 figures from Nakamura Takafusa, *Economic growth in prewar Japan*, Yale University Press, New Haven, (1983), p. 207. 1946–52 figures from Office of the Prime Minister, Bureau of Statistics, *Japan statistical yearbook, 1953*, Office of the Prime Minister, Tokyo. (1953), pp. 280–3.

Appendix II Measures of 'Overloan', 1900–51

	Loans: deposits + capital	Borrowings from Bank of Japan: Total funds employed[a]
	'Ordinary' banks	
1900	93%	12%
1910	78	2
1920	84	2
1930	64	2
1940	53	1
	All banks[b]	
1945	73	22
1946	74	19
1947	71	9
1948	80	9
1949	92	10
1950	102	14
1951	108	17
	'City' banks	
1945	94	29
1946	124	28
1947	83	14
1948	85	13
1949	98	13
1950	117	19
1951	124	25

Notes: a. Total funds employed = capital + deposits + borrowings from the Bank of Japan.
b. Includes 'ordinary' banks, savings banks and government financial institutions.
Source: Suzuki Yoshio, *Money and banking in contemporary Japan*, Yale University Press, New Haven, (1980), pp. 10–11.

Notes

CHAPTER 1

1. Hugh Patrick, 'Japan, 1868–1914' in Rondo Cameron (ed.), *Banking in the early stages of industrialization* (Oxford University Press, New York, 1967), p. 288.

2. Quoted from the correspondence of Matsukata in Yoshino Toshihiko, 'The creation of the Bank of Japan — its Western origin and adaptation', *The Developing Economies* XV, no. 3 (September 1977), p. 385.

3. Patrick, 'Japan, 1868–1914', p. 251.

4. Fuji Bank Ltd, *Banking in modern Japan*, 2nd edn (Fuji Bank, Tokyo, 1967), pp. 33–4.

5. Ibid., p. 54.

6. Nakamura Takafusa, *Economic growth in prewar Japan*, (trans. R.A. Feldman) (Yale University Press, New Haven, 1983), p. 302.

7. Yamamura Kozo, 'Japan, 1868–1930: a revised view' in Rondo Cameron (ed.), *Banking and economic development* (Oxford University Press, New York, 1972), p. 194.

8. Many definitions of 'overloan' exist, though all describe what is essentially the same condition. Suzuki Yoshio provides a thorough economic analysis of 'overloan' in *Money and banking in contemporary Japan* (Yale University Press, New Haven, 1980).

9. Widespread 'overloan' disappeared in Japan as more funds were generated within the system and banking standards were gradually improved. Asakura Kokichi, 'The characteristics of finance in the Meiji period (the period of take-off)', *The Developing Economies* V, no. 2 (June 1967), p. 290. See also Appendix II.

10. In many cases, shares purchased by individuals were used as collateral for loans which were, in turn, used to purchase even more shares. Bank credit was so used to fund most individual subscriptions to corporate stock. Patrick, 'Japan, 1868–1914', pp. 282–4.

11. Fuji Bank, *Banking in modern Japan*, pp. 107–8.

12. Phra Sarasas, *Money and banking in Japan* (Heath Cranton, London, 1940), p. 113.

13. Edna Ehrlich, 'The role of banking in Japan's economic development' (unpublished PhD dissertation, The New School for Social Research, 1960), p. 83.

14. In 1894, for example, 40 per cent of ordinary bank loans were for a term of over one year. Patrick, 'Japan, 1868–1914', pp. 280–2.

15. Ibid., p. 288.

16. The structure, history and significance of the *zaibatsu* have been widely documented in English. A standard source is Eleanor Hadley's *Antitrust in Japan* (Princeton University Press, Princeton, 1970).

17. Nakamura, *Economic growth*, p. 210.

18. Mission on Japanese Combines, *Report, Part 1* (Department of State Publication 2628, Far Eastern Series 14, Washington, 1946), p. 50.

19. See Appendix I for further statistical information on banking concentration.

20. Fuji Bank, *Banking in modern Japan*, pp. 103–5.

21. Raymond Goldsmith, *The financial development of Japan, 1968–1977* (Yale University Press, New Haven, 1983), p. 89.

22. Fuji Bank, *Banking in modern Japan*, pp. 34–5.

23. Patrick, 'Japan, 1868–1914', pp. 268–70.

24. Goldsmith, *Financial development*, p. 86.

25. Patrick, 'Japan, 1868–1914', p. 272.

26. Ibid., p. 249; Bank of Japan, Economic Research Department, *Money and banking in Japan*, L.S. Pressnell (ed.), S. Nishimura (trans.) (Macmillan, London, 1973), p. 11.

27. Fuji Bank, *Banking in modern Japan*, p. 97.

28. Goldsmith, *Financial development*, p. 83.

29. Fuji Bank, *Banking in modern Japan*, p. 84.

30. A detailed description of the crisis is provided in Cho Yukio, 'Exposing the incompetence of the bourgeoisie: the financial panic of 1927', *Japan Interpreter* 8, no. 4 (Winter 1974), pp. 492–501.

31. Quoted in Cho, 'Exposing the incompetence', p. 501.

32. Fuji Bank, *Banking in modern Japan*, pp. 98–9.

33. Hugh Patrick, 'The economic muddle of the 1920s' in J.W. Morley (ed.), *Dilemmas of growth in prewar Japan* (Princeton University Press, Princeton, 1971), p. 242.

34. Ehrlich, 'The role of banking', p. 97.

35. Fuji Bank, *Banking in modern Japan*, p. 97.

36. Sakurai Kinichiro, *Financial aspects of economic development of Japan* (Science Council of Japan, Economic Series 34, Tokyo, 1964), pp. 139–41; a contemporary view is presented by Phra Sarasas, *Money and banking*, p. 297.

37. Fuji Bank, *Banking in modern Japan*, p. 127.

38. Mitsui Bank, *A history of the first 100 years* (Mitsui Bank Ltd, Tokyo, 1976), p. 106.

39. Mission on Japanese Combines, *Report*, p. 37.

40. Fuji Bank, *Banking in modern Japan*, p. 137.

41. Kawaguchi Hiroshi, 'The "dual structure" of finance in post-war Japan', *The Developing Economies* V, no. 2 (June 1967), p. 302; Fuji Bank, *Banking in modern Japan*, p. 141.

42. Johannes Hirschmeier and Yui Tsunehiko, *The development of Japanese business: 1600–1980*, 2nd edn (George Allen and Unwin, London, 1981), p. 235.

43. Fuji Bank, *Banking in modern Japan*, p. 141.

44. Goldsmith, *Financial development*, pp. 125–7.

45. Commercial bank advances increased only eightfold during the same period (1936–45). Bank of Japan, *Money and banking*, p. 40.

46. Fuji Bank, *Banking in modern Japan*, pp. 160–1.

47. By 1944, government organisations controlled over 50 per cent of total assets in Japanese financial institutions. Goldsmith, *Financial development*, p. 122.

48. R.B. Rice, 'Hitachi: Japanese industry in an era of militarism, 1937–1945' (unpublished PhD dissertation, Harvard University, 1974), p. 244.

49. Jerome Cohen, *Japan's economy in the war and reconstruction* (University of Minnesota Press, Minneapolis, 1949), p. 85.

50. Ibid., p. 20.

51. Bank of Japan Law (Law no. 67, 24 February 1942), Chapter I, Article 2, in *Japanese laws relating to banks* (EHS Law Series, vol. VI, Eibun Horei-sha, Tokyo, 1976), p. AA1.

52. Bank of Japan Law, Chapter I, Article 1, ibid.

53. Bank of Japan Law, Chapter III, Article 25, ibid., p. AA8.

54. Bank of Japan Law, Chapter VI, ibid., pp. AA12–AA13.

55. Cohen, *Japan's economy*, pp. 16–17.

56. Fuji Bank, *Banking in modern Japan*, pp. 140–1.

57. Takahashi Makoto, 'The development of war-time economic controls', *The Developing Economies* V, no. 4 (December 1967), p. 651.

58. Fuji Bank, *Banking in modern Japan*, pp. 159–60.

59. Ibid., pp. 162–3.

60. Cohen, *Japan's economy*, p. 91.

61. Fuji Bank, *Banking in modern Japan*, p. 167.

CHAPTER 2

1. Quoted in John Dower, *Empire and aftermath* (Harvard East Asian Monographs 84, Cambridge, 1979), p. 278.

2. SCAP, *Political reorientation of Japan* (2 vols, Greenwood Press Reprint, Westport, Conn., 1970), vol. II, p. 785.

3. US Department of State, *Postwar foreign policy preparation, 1939–45* (GPO, Washington, February 1950), p. 371.

4. SCAP, *Political reorientation*, vol. II, p. 425.

5. The experience in Occupied Germany was much the same. Deviation from the highly punitive 'Morgenthau Plan' was necessary to prevent economic collapse. John Backer, 'From Morgenthau Plan to Marshall Plan' in Robert Wolfe (ed.), *Americans as proconsuls* (Southern Illinois University Press, Carbondale, 1984), pp. 157–8.

6. Yoshida Shigeru, *The Yoshida memoirs*, Yoshida Kenichi (trans.), (Heinemann, London, 1961), p. 128.

7. T.J. Pempel, 'The tar baby target: "reform" of the Japanese bureaucracy' in Robert Ward and Sakamoto Yoshikazu (eds) *Democratizing Japan* (University of Hawaii Press, Honolulu, 1987), pp. 163–4, 173–4.

8. MacArthur's civil headquarters was divided on a functional basis into 'sections', composed of various 'divisions', which in turn were made up of 'branches', sometimes further subdivided into 'units'.

9. Theodore Cohen, *Remaking Japan: the American Occupation as new deal*, Herbert Passin (ed.) (Free Press, New York, 1987), p. 10.

10. Ibid., p. 81.

11. W. Macmahon Ball, *Japan . . . enemy or ally* (Cassell, London, 1948), pp. 22–3.

12. Cable, ESS to War Department, 14 October 1945, Records of Allied Operational and Occupation Headquarters, World War II (SCAP archives), Washington National Records Center (hereafter referred to as SCAP-WNRC), Record Group (RG) 331 Box 6384.

13. Harry Emerson Wildes, *Typhoon in Tokyo* (George Allen and Unwin, London, 1954), pp. 8–10; Mark Gayn, *Japan diary* (Charles Tuttle, Rutland, Vt., 1981), pp. 339–41.

14. A participant's view of SCAP recruitment is given in Cohen, *Remaking Japan*, pp. 104–5.

15. ESS-FI memorandum for record, 1 December 1945, SCAP-WNRC, RG331 Box 7567.

16. Cable, ESS to War Department, 14 October 1945, SCAP-WNRC, RG331 Box 6384.

17. In JCS 1380/15, the November 1945 Joint Chiefs of Staff basic directive to MacArthur, the occupiers were enjoined to close special wartime financial institutions, take control of foreign exchange transactions and block the assets of militarist societies and organisations. Otherwise, Washington only instructed that 'in the financial field, you [SCAP] will make full application of the principles stated elsewhere in this directive'. US Department of State, *A decade of American foreign policy, 1941–49* (GPO, Washington, 1950), pp. 648–52.

18. SCAP Historical Monograph 39 (vol. XIII — Finance, Part C), *Money and banking*, 30 November 1951, SCAP-WNRC, p. 1.

19. JCS 1380/15, transmitted to SCAP 3 November 1945, in SCAP, *Political reorientation*, vol. II, pp. 437–9.

20. Ibid., p. 435.

21. Memorandum, Sherbourne (ESS-FI, M&B) to Thomas, 23 October 1945, SCAP-WNRC, RG331 Box 7567.

22. John Backer, *Priming the German economy* (Duke University Press, Durham, 1971), pp. 90–3. Joseph Dodge was one of the principal architects of the German currency reform.

23. Memorandum, Sherbourne to Thomas, 23 October 1945, SCAP-WNRC, RG331 Box 7567.

24. Sharon Nolte, *Liberalism in modern Japan: Ishibashi Tanzan and his teachers, 1905–1960* (University of California Press, Berkeley, 1987), pp. 293–4.

25. Chalmers Johnson, *MITI and the Japanese miracle* (University of California Press, Berkeley, 1982), pp. 177–8.

26. Memorandum, ESS-FI to Economic Advisor, ESS, 12 February 1947, SCAP-WNRC, RG331 Box 8356.

27. SCAP controls are discussed in Leon Hollerman, 'International economic controls in Occupied Japan', *Journal of Asian Studies* XXXVIII, no. 4 (August 1979).

28. *The Oriental Economist*, 9 February 1946, pp. 70–1.

29. *The Oriental Economist*, 2 March 1946, p. 119.

30. Some authors have noted that the Japanese programme was more favourable to the reconstruction of commercial banking than the German currency reform of 1948 proved to be, particularly in that deposits were blocked and currency converted in a 1:1 ratio. See Kent Calder, 'Politics and the market: the dynamics of Japanese credit allocation, 1946–78' (unpublished PhD dissertation, Harvard University, 1979), p. 110n.

31. *The Oriental Economist*, 23 March 1946, p. 170.

32. *The Oriental Economist*, 2 February 1946, p. 56.

33. Dick K. Nanto, 'The United States' role in the postwar economic

recovery of Japan' (unpublished PhD dissertation, Harvard University, 1976), p. 208.

34. Memorandum, Sherbourne to Thomas, 23 October 1945, SCAP-WNRC, RG331 Box 7567.

35. Fuji Bank, *Banking in modern Japan*, p. 191.

36. Ibid., p. 190.

37. 'Remarks by Mr. T.E. Beplat, Chief, Money and Banking Branch, ESS-FI', Allied Council for Japan, 16 April 1947, SCAP-WNRC, RG331 Box 6323.

38. Fuji Bank, *Banking in modern Japan*, p. 191.

39. 'Remarks by Mr. T.E. Beplat', Allied Council for Japan.

40. Parallel statutes to guide the reorganisation of industrial and commercial firms and insurance companies were enacted at the same time.

41. SCAP Historical Monograph 39, pp. 21–2.

42. 'Reorganization of the Teikoku Bank', ESS-FI, M&B memorandum for file, 21 March 1947, SCAP-WNRC, RG331 Box 7567.

43. 'Major post surrender legislation affecting the zaibatsu', undated SCAP study, Records of the Under Secretary of the Army — WNRC, RG335 Box 51, p. 9.

44. Fuji Bank, *Banking in modern Japan*, p. 212.

45. Ibid., pp. 191–2.

46. Ibid., p. 212.

47. JCS 1380/15, SCAP, *Political reorientation*, vol. II, p. 437.

48. ESS-FI, 'Report on political and economic conditions in Japan', September 1947, SCAP-WNRC, RG331 Box 8356.

49. Ibid.

50. It has also been suggested that SCAP sought abolition of the 'special' banks in order to promote the 'orthodox concept' of raising industrial investment funds through equity finance (rather than long-term bank loans). Industrial Bank, *Long-term credit banking system of Japan* (Industrial Bank, Tokyo, 1957), p. 5. While this assertion appears reasonable in light of SCAP's overall policy aims, no documentary evidence has been offered to support this interpretation.

51. SCAP Historical Monograph 39, pp. 16–17.

52. Chalmers Johnson, *Japan's public policy companies* (American Enterprise Institute, Washington, 1978), pp. 87–8.

53. Calder, 'Politics and the market', pp. 68–9.

54. Ibid., p. 68.

55. SCAPIN 863, SCAP Historical Monograph 39, appendices.

56. Memorandum, ESS-FI to Economic Advisor, ESS, 12 February 1947, SCAP-WNRC, RG331 Box 8356.

57. Calder, 'Politics and the market', pp. 166–8.

58. ESS-FI, M&B memorandum for file, 11 July 1947, SCAP-WNRC, RG331 Box 7567.

59. Calder, 'Politics and the market', pp. 170–1.

60. Yoshida, *Memoirs*, p. 288.

61. Memorandum, ESS-FI to Chief, ESS, 5 June 1946, SCAP-WNRC, RG331 Box 6384.

CHAPTER 3

1. Quoted in Basil Rausch, *The history of the New Deal 1933–1938*, 2nd edn (Octagon Books, New York, 1980), pp. 252–3.

2. Cohen, *Remaking Japan*, p. 47.

3. General Douglas MacArthur, 'Reply to criticism of economic policy', 24 January 1948, in SCAP, *Political reorientation*, vol. II, p. 781.

4. Mission on Japanese Combines, *Report*, p. vii.

5. Corwin Edwards, 'The dissolution of the Japanese combines', *Pacific Affairs* XIX, no. 3 (September 1946), pp. 228–9.

6. The best study of the pre-surrender planning in Washington is Marlene Mayo's 'American economic planning for Occupied Japan: the issue of *zaibatsu* dissolution' in Lawrence Redford (ed.), *The Occupation of Japan: economic policy and reform* (The MacArthur Memorial, Norfolk, Virginia, 1980), pp. 205–28.

7. SCAP, *Political reorientation*, vol. II, p. 425.

8. On a superficial level, major *zaibatsu* affiliates — including the banks — changed their corporate names in an attempt to distance themselves (at least in the occupiers' eyes) from the combines. cf. Hosoya Masahiro, 'Selected aspects of zaibatsu dissolution in Occupied Japan, 1945–52' (unpublished PhD dissertation, Yale University, 1982), pp. 186–214.

9. Ibid., pp. 44–7.

10. T.A. Bisson, *Zaibatsu dissolution in Japan* (Greenwood Press, Westport, 1976), Appendix 2 (the Yasuda Plan), pp. 241–4.

11. Ibid., p. 75.

12. Quoted in Hosoya, 'Zaibatsu dissolution', pp. 49–50.

13. Ibid., pp. 106–7.

14. Mission on Japanese Combines, *Report*, p. x.

15. Ibid.

16. Quoted in Hosoya, 'Zaibatsu dissolution', p. 115.

17. Ibid., p. 114.

18. Quoted in Hadley, *Antitrust*, Appendix IX, p. 498.

19. JCS 1380/15, 3 November 1945. SCAP, *Political reorientation*, vol. II, p. 435.

20. Memorandum, signed E.C. Sherbourne, 19 November 1945, SCAP-WNRC, RG331 Box 7567.

21. Edwards, 'Dissolution', p. 233.

22. Mission on Japanese Combines, *Report*, p. 48.

23. Mission on Japanese Combines, 'Summary of recommendations', SCAP-WNRC, RG331 Box 8356.

24. SCAP-GHQ, 'Comments on the report of the Edwards Mission', undated, SCAP-WNRC, RG331 Box 8356.

25. Hadley, *Antitrust*, pp. 73–6.

26. Ibid., pp. 164–5.

27. Quoted in Hosoya, 'Zaibatsu dissolution', p. 79.

28. Memorandum, Chief, ESS-FI to Marquat, 2 December 1947, SCAP-WNRC, RG331 Box 5976.

29. Ibid.

30. Many in SCAP found Welsh abrasive. Ted Cohen described him as stubborn and inflexible, 'strong willed yet narrowly focused'. His long

memoranda were legendary and Cohen tagged the ESS-A/C Chief 'the man of a few thousand Welsh chosen words'. Cohen, *Remaking Japan*, pp. 352, 365.

31. Hadley, *Antitrust*, Appendix IX, p. 505.

32. Hosoya, 'Zaibatsu dissolution', p. 119.

33. ESS-A/C, 'Standards for excessive concentrations in banking fields', 10 January 1948, SCAP-WNRC, RG331 Box 8468.

34. Cf. Cohen, *Remaking Japan*, p. 363. Cohen described Welsh's standards as 'vague', 'arbitrary' and 'unreal'.

35. ESS-A/C, 'Standards for excessive concentrations in banking fields', 10 January 1948, SCAP-WNRC, RG331 Box 8468.

36. Hosoya, 'Zaibatsu dissolution', pp. 121–4.

37. Bisson, *Zaibatsu dissolution*, Appendix 5 (Law 207), pp. 262–8.

38. Cable, MacArthur to Army Department, 26 January 1948, Records of the Under Secretary of the Army — WNRC, RG335 Box 52.

39. Ibid.

40. Memorandum, Kupferer (Deputy Chief, ESS-A/C) to Chief, Research Division, 18 December 1946, SCAP-WNRC, RG331 Box 8468.

41. Summary of ESS-A/C Staff Study (Research Division Report), 'Banking reorganization', 9 February 1948, SCAP-WNRC, RG331 Box 8468.

42. Ibid.

43. Ibid.

44. Ibid.

45. Tristan Beplat, 'Banking and deconcentration' in Redford (ed.), *The Occupation of Japan*, p. 237.

46. See Appendix I.

47. Memorandum, LeCount to Chief, ESS, 19 February 1948, SCAP-WNRC, RG331 Box 8468.

48. Ibid.

49. Ibid.

50. Beplat, 'Banking and deconcentration', pp. 237–8.

51. J.S.G. Wilson, *Banking policy and structure* (Croom Helm, London, 1986), p. 155.

52. Hans Adler, 'The post-war reorganization of the German banking system', *Quarterly Journal of Economics* LXIII, no. 3 (April 1949), p. 341. German feelings on economic concentration apparently mirrored Japanese: 'Germany has never known anything like the fear and resentment that monopoly used to arouse in the United States . . . Unrestricted competition is usually referred to as "destructive" . . . Many Germans find it difficult to believe that something growing up without order and control, like a competitive market, could not be improved by a little discipline.' Henry C. Wallich, *Mainsprings of the German revival* (Yale University Press, New Haven, 1955), pp. 136–7.

53. Andrew Shonfield, *Modern capitalism* (Oxford University Press for the Royal Institute of International Affairs, London, 1965), pp. 241–2.

54. Memorandum, LeCount to Chief, ESS, 16 March 1948, SCAP-WNRC, RG331 Box 8468.

55. Memorandum, LeCount to Chief, ESS, 20 April 1948, SCAP-WNRC, RG331 Box 8468.

56. A firsthand description of how a similar divisional dispute (in labour

policy) was settled through the intervention of MacArthur is given by Alfred Oppler in his *Legal reform in Occupied Japan* (Princeton University Press, Princeton, 1976), p. 206. Cohen also notes two cases of interdivisional debate resolved by Marquat's intercession. Cohen, *Remaking Japan*, pp. 184, 390.

57. Pempel concluded that 'In analyzing the internal memoranda of the Occupation, one is forced to ask just what percentage of top officials [was] devoted to "reforming Japan" and what percentage to resolving jurisdictional disputes by elements of the Occupation arguing about their respective spheres of responsibility for such reforms'. Pempel, 'The tar baby target', p. 174.

58. Memorandum, LeCount to Chief, ESS, 20 April 1948, SCAP-WNRC, RG331 Box 8468.

59. Cohen has stated that the Supreme Commander was sympathetic to 'trust busting', especially in the case of the *zaibatsu* banks: 'MacArthur had a populist's distrust of big finance. He could tolerate bigness in industry, for he could see the material results, and he was proud of American big business productivity, but financial institutions were too prone to exploit the little man.' Cohen, *Remaking Japan*, p. 371.

60. George Kennan, *Memoirs, 1925-50* (Atlantic Monthly Press, Boston, 1967), p. 368.

61. Quoted in J. Livingston, J. Moore and F. Oldfather (eds), *Postwar Japan* (Pantheon, New York, 1973), pp. 117-19.

62. Cohen, *Remaking Japan*, p. 404.

63. *Newsweek*, 1 December 1947, pp. 36-8.

64. Walter Mills (ed.), *The Forrestal diaries* (Viking Press, New York, 1951), p. 328.

65. Quoted in Hadley, *Antitrust*, p. 137.

66. The delegation was officially led by Johnston (and hence was also known as the 'Johnston Mission'), while Draper only 'accompanied' it. Nevertheless, Draper was clearly the guiding influence in the group and took most of the responsibility for drafting the final report.

67. Memorandum for record, ESS-A/C, 22 April 1948, SCAP-WNRC, RG331 Box 5979; Hosoya, 'Zaibatsu dissolution', pp. 174-5.

68. Memorandum, LeCount to Chief, ESS, 28 April 1948, SCAP-WNRC, RG331 Box 5979.

69. Memorandum for record, ESS, 18 April 1948, SCAP-WNRC, RG331 Box 5976.

70. Memorandum, LeCount to Chief, ESS, 23 April 1948, SCAP-WNRC, RG331 Box 8468.

71. Ibid.

72. Memorandum, Welsh to Chief, ESS, 26 April 1948, SCAP-WNRC, RG331 Box 5976.

73. Notes signed Edward Welsh on memorandum, LeCount to Chief, ESS, 23 April 1948, SCAP-WNRC, RG331 Box 8468.

74. Memorandum, Chief, Legal Section to Marquat, 1 May 1948, SCAP-WNRC, RG331 Box 5976.

75. Memorandum, signed Welsh, 7 July 1948, SCAP-WNRC, RG331 Box 8468.

76. Hosoya, 'Zaibatsu dissolution', p. 182.

77. Memorandum, Marquat to Chief of Staff, 26 May 1948, SCAP-WNRC, RG331 Box 5976.

78. Cable, Draper to MacArthur, 6 May 1948, SCAP-WNRC, RG331 Box 5976.

79. According to Ted Cohen, Marquat would sometimes vacillate in inter-divisional disputes so as to avoid making hard decisions on issues which he did not have the economic skill to analyse adequately. This is perhaps the best explanation for Marquat's inconsistent positions on the banking deconcentration issue. Cf. Cohen, *Remaking Japan*, p. 180.

80. Memorandum, DRB to SCAP, 2 July 1948, Records of the Under Secretary of the Army — WNRC, RG335 Box 52.

81. Ibid.

82. Memorandum, signed Welsh, 7 July 1948, SCAP-WNRC, RG331 Box 8468.

83. Personal letter, Welsh to Marquat, 18 July 1948, SCAP-WNRC, RG331 Box 8468.

84. Memorandum, signed Welsh, 30 July 1948, SCAP-WNRC, RG331 Box 5976; Draft Press Release, HCLC, 29 July 1948, SCAP-WNRC, RG331 Box 8468.

85. Memorandum, Raymond Vernon to Paul Nitze, 'Present status of the zaibatsu program in Japan', 30 September 1948, Records of the Far Eastern Commission — US Delegation File, Diplomatic Section, National Archives, Washington, RG43 Box 220.

86. R.N. Rosecrance, *Australian diplomacy and Japan, 1945–1951* (Cambridge University Press, London, 1962), pp. 164–5; *Nippon Times*, 10 March 1950.

87. *Nippon Times*, 10 March 1950.

88. Memorandum, Welsh to Allison (Acting Director of Finance, ESS), 11 March 1950, SCAP-WNRC, RG331 Box 5976.

89. Press Release: 'A statement on Japanese banking', Far East Command GHQ, Public Information Section, SCAP-WNRC, RG331 Box 5976.

CHAPTER 4

1. Mission on Japanese Combines, *Report*, p. 51; Fuji Bank, *Banking in modern Japan*, pp. 225–7.

2. Memorandum, LeCount to Chief, ESS, 2 December 1947, SCAP-WNRC, RG331 Box 5976; Fuji Bank, *Banking in modern Japan*, pp. 225–7.

3. The term 'city banks' has been widely used in the postwar years to refer to the small group of very large banks which operate on a national (and international) scale. The *zaibatsu* institutions are classed as 'city banks'.

4. Beplat, 'Banking and deconcentration', p. 238.

5. The Kyowa Bank, for example, was the reorganised successor to the Japan Savings Bank, largest of the thrift institutions, and has emerged in the postwar years as one of the 'city banks'.

6. Beplat, 'Banking and deconcentration', p. 240.

7. Wildes, *Typhoon*, p. 26.

8. Mission on Japanese Combines, *Report*, pp. 53–9.

9. Ibid., p. 53.

10. Mission on Japanese Combines, 'Summary of recommendations', SCAP-WNRC, RG331 Box 8356.

11. SCAP-GHQ, 'Comments on the report of the Edwards Mission', SCAP-WNRC, RG331 Box 8356.

12. Hadley, *Antitrust*, Appendix IX, p. 506.

13. The banks were, however, subject to ESS-A/C's Antimonopoly Law, which included several provisions targeted specifically at financial institutions. Under the 1947 statute, in addition to the general regulations on interlocking directorates, mergers and competitive practices, the banks were subject to special limitations on the proportion of a corporation's total stock or bond issues which could be held. These regulations ultimately had little real effect on the banks' operations.

14. More information on the Federal Reserve programme is detailed in Arthur Bloomfield and John Jensen, *Banking reform in South Korea* (Federal Reserve Bank of New York, New York, 1951).

15. 'Remarks by Mr. T.E. Beplat', Allied Council for Japan.

16. Memorandum, LeCount to Chief, ESS, 8 March 1948, SCAP-WNRC, RG331 Box 8468.

17. Ibid.

18. Ibid.

19. Memorandum, LeCount to Chief, ESS, 2 December 1947, SCAP-WNRC, RG331 Box 5976.

20. Memorandum, LeCount to Chief, ESS, 28 May 1948, SCAP-WNRC, RG331 Box 7691.

21. Ibid.

22. Ibid.

23. Ibid.

24. Ibid.

25. An overview of the contemporary American system is presented in US Board of Governors of the Federal Reserve System, *The Federal Reserve System*, R. Young (ed.), (Washington, 1954).

26. Cagle was, no doubt, influenced by the active debate over the authority and independence of the Federal Reserve Board which raged in the United States during the late 1940s. Cagle must have hoped to prevent a similar situation in Japan by making the Banking Board's prerogatives and position *vis-à-vis* the central government unambiguous. An overview of the US debate is given in J.S. Fforde, *The Federal Reserve System, 1945–49* (The Clarendon Press, Oxford, 1954).

27. Memorandum, LeCount to Chief, ESS, 28 May 1948, SCAP-WNRC, RG331 Box 7691.

28. It is noteworthy that Edwards had recommended full government ownership of the Bank of Japan. The ESS-FI decision to seek the transfer of Bank ownership entirely to the private sector reflects that division's particular interpretation of the development of Japanese finance under militarism. To the ESS-FI planners, politicised bureaucrats were a much greater potential threat to 'economic democracy' than established business interests and central bank ownership was thus more safely vested in the private sector than in the government.

29. The existing Board of Directors was a non-representative body without the ability to exert direct, 'democratic' influence over Bank policy. The so-called 'directors' were executive officers of the Bank appointed by the Minister of Finance.

30. Memorandum, LeCount to Chief, ESS, 28 May 1948, SCAP-WNRC, RG331 Box 7691.

31. Ibid.

32. Under the Securities and Exchange Law of April 1948, designed in the Securities Division of the ESS and enacted under American pressure, the banks were barred from underwriting securities other than government issues. While this statute did not end the banks' important role in absorbing securities, it did give a boost to independent securities firms by breaking the traditional dominance of the *zaibatsu* banks in underwriting. Cf. T.F.M. Adams and Hoshii Iwao, *A financial history of the new Japan* (Kodansha International, Tokyo, 1972), pp. 51–2.

33. Memorandum, LeCount to Chief, ESS, 28 May 1948, SCAP-WNRC, RG331 Box 7691.

34. Memorandum, Welsh to Chief, ESS, 23 April 1948, SCAP-WNRC, RG331 Box 8468.

35. ESS-A/C Staff Study, 'Banking reorganization', undated, SCAP-WNRC, RG331 Box 8468.

36. Memorandum, Welsh to ESS-FI, 2 August 1948, SCAP-WNRC, RG331 Box 8468.

37. Mr Loree of the Draper Mission and the members of the Young Mission (studying the yen-dollar exchange rate) were apparently supportive of the proposed legal reform; memorandum, Cagle to LeCount, 8 December 1948, SCAP-WNRC, RG331 Box 5976.

38. Draft memorandum by ESS-FI, 15 July 1948, SCAP-WNRC, RG331 Box 8468.

39. Memorandum, Cagle to LeCount, 8 December 1948, SCAP-WNRC, RG331 Box 5976.

40. The development of the stabilisation programme is outlined in W.M. Tsutsui, 'Stabilization and reconstruction in Japan, 1945–50' (unpublished A.B. thesis, Harvard College, 1985).

41. Cable, Draper to SCAP, 27 October 1948, SCAP-WNRC, RG331 Box 5976.

42. Ibid.

43. Cable, SCAP to Army Department, 4 October 1948, SCAP-WNRC, RG331 Box 539.

44. Memorandum for record by Cagle, 26 November 1948, SCAP-WNRC, RG331 Box 5976.

45. Memorandum, LeCount to Chief, ESS, 17 December 1948, SCAP-WNRC, RG331 Box 5976.

46. Bloomfield and Jensen, *Banking reform*, p. 5.

47. Cable, Draper to SCAP, 15 December 1948, Records of the Under Secretary of the Army — WNRC, RG335 Box 52.

48. Memorandum, Cagle to LeCount, 28 December 1948, SCAP-WNRC, RG331 Box 7691.

49. Memorandum, LeCount to Chief, ESS, 31 December 1948, SCAP-WNRC, RG331 Box 7691.

50. Cable, SCAP to Army Department, 14 February 1949, SCAP-WNRC, RG331 Box 539.

51. Bank of Japan Law, as amended 3 June 1949, Chapters I–II, *Japanese laws relating to banks*, pp. AA2–3.

52. Cable, SCAP to Army Department (personal Dodge to Draper), 21 February 1949, SCAP-WNRC, RG331 Box 539.

53. Cable, Army Department to SCAP, 25 February 1949, SCAP-WNRC, RG331 Box 539.

54. Cable, Army Department to SCAP, 5 March 1949, SCAP-WNRC, RG331 Box 539; memorandum of conversation, Dodge and Governor Ichimada of Bank of Japan, 1 April 1949, Joseph M. Dodge Papers, Burton Historical Collection, Detroit Public Library (hereafter referred to as Dodge Ms.), Japan 1949 Box 6.

55. Bank of Japan Law, *Japanese laws relating to banks*, pp. AA1–22.

56. Letter, Dodge to Marquat, 16 June 1950, Dodge Ms., Japan 1950 Box 7.

57. Letter, Dodge to R. Reid (Department of the Treasury), 7 March 1951, Dodge Ms., Japan 1951 Box 2.

58. *The Oriental Economist*, 9 July 1949, p. 651.

59. This is discussed further in Chapter 5; memorandum for file, Martin Bronfenbrenner (Internal Revenue Division, ESS), 20 April 1950, Dodge Ms., Japan 1950 Box 2; letter, Marquat to Dodge, 13 May 1950, Dodge Ms., Japan 1950 Box 3.

60. Memorandum, Paul Moody Atkins (consultant economist to SCAP on banking statistics) to Marquat, 25 October 1948, SCAP-WNRC, RG331 Box 5976.

61. Memorandum for record by Cagle, 26 November 1948, SCAP-WNRC, RG331 Box 5976.

62. Report on 'Legal reforms in banking' presented to Dodge by 'All-Japan Local Banks Association', 22 December 1951, Dodge Ms., Japan 1951 Box 1. The proposed concentration of power in the Ministry of Finance would apparently have upset the existing balance in bureaucracy-banking relations. Bank of Japan and private-sector opposition was not to bureaucratic intervention *per se* but to the substantial increase in government supervision and Finance Ministry discretionary authority which the proposed revision seemed to promise.

63. Letter, Dodge to Reid, 12 November 1950, Dodge Ms., Japan 1950 Box 2.

CHAPTER 5

1. Martin Bronfenbrenner, 'Four positions on Japanese finance', *Journal of Political Economy*, LVIII, no. 4 (August 1950), p. 286.

2. Sherwood Fine, 'Japan's postwar industrial recovery', *Contemporary Japan*, XXI, nos. 4–6 (1952), p. 182. Fine was Director of Finance and Economics in SCAP from 1949 to 1952.

3. The extent of government subsidisation is documented in Edward Hutchinson, 'Inflation and stabilization in postwar Japan' (unpublished PhD dissertation, University of Virginia, 1954), p. 156.

4. Adams and Hoshii, *Financial history*, p. 35.

5. Martin Bronfenbrenner, 'Economic policy under MacArthur', *United Asia*, 3, no. 4 (1951), p. 250.

6. Tsuru Shigeto, 'Toward economic stability in Japan', *Pacific Affairs*, 22 (December 1949), p. 362.

7. From 1945 until 1949, Japan's overseas trade was administered entirely through official channels and under the close regulation of SCAP. Without a stable structure of exchange rates, the system resembled barter, with the Japanese government essentially underwriting most foreign transactions. 'If the Japanese Government purchased export goods on the domestic economy for an amount of yen, A, and sold them abroad for, say, B amount of dollars, the yen/dollar rate for those goods could only be calculated retroactively as one dollar = (A/B) yen. The process for imports was the reverse. Thus there were complicated exchange rates for each item of trade.' Nakamura Takafusa, *The postwar Japanese economy* (Tokyo University Press, Tokyo, 1981), p. 36. In maintaining this system, the official subsidisation of virtually all import and export transactions was inevitable.

8. Bronfenbrenner, 'Economic policy under MacArthur', p. 250.

9. Percy Johnston and others, 'Report' (26 April 1948), SCAP-WNRC, RG331 Box 5982.

10. Ralph Young and others, 'Report on the special mission on yen foreign exchange policy' (21 June 1948), SCAP-WNRC, RG331 Box 5981.

11. Cable, SCAP to Draper, 13 June 1948, SCAP-WNRC, RG331 Box 5981.

12. The other members of the Dodge Mission were Orville McDiarmid (State Department), Ralph Reid (Army), W.W. Diehl (Treasury), Paul O'Leary (Cornell University), Audley Stephan (Rutgers University). Soong Hoom Kil, 'The Dodge Line and the Japanese Conservative Party' (unpublished PhD dissertation, University of Michigan, 1977), p. 78.

13. Cohen, *Remaking Japan*, p. 432.

14. General Marquat carried on an extensive personal correspondence with Dodge from 1949 until the end of the Occupation. Virtually all major SCAP economic decisions were 'unofficially' cleared by the Financial Advisor through this channel.

15. Cf. 'Biographical sketch of Joseph Dodge', unsigned, Dodge Ms.

16. Statement by Joseph Dodge, 7 March 1949, in Japan, Foreign Office, *Documents concerning the allied occupation and control of Japan*, vol. III (Tokyo, August 1949), pp. 30-3.

17. Dodge, 'Statement on the Japanese budget', 15 April 1949, in *Contemporary Japan*, XVII, nos 4-6 (April-June 1949), pp. 269-74.

18. The most comprehensive economic analysis of the inflation is presented by Nanto, 'The United States' role', and confirms that deficit spending was the force behind the inflation.

19. Dodge, statement, 7 March 1949, p. 30.

20. Jerome Cohen, *Japan's postwar economy* (Indiana University Press, Bloomington, 1958), p. 87.

21. Kil, 'The Dodge Line', p. 96.

22. Letter, W.W. Diehl to Dodge, 18 February 1949, Dodge Ms., Japan 1949 Box 1.

23. Cable, Dodge to Army Department, 19 February 1949, Dodge Ms., Japan 1949 Box 1.

24. Letter, Kudo Shoshiro (Vice-president, RFB) to Diehl, 27 July 1949, Dodge Ms., Japan 1949 Box 2.

25. Ibid., handwritten notes in margin by Dodge.

26. Dodge, statement, 15 April 1949, p. 274.

27. Ibid.

28. Ibid., p. 273.

29. Nanto, 'The United States' role', p. 261.

30. Dodge, statement, 7 March 1949, p. 33.

31. Ted Cohen explained: 'If [Dodge] detested excessive government participation in commerce and industry . . . it was because he thought it inefficient and therefore a burdensome hidden tax on the economy, holding back its recovery.' Cohen, *Remaking Japan*, p. 433.

32. Orville McDiarmid, 'The Dodge and Young Missions' and comments by Martin Bronfenbrenner in Redford (ed.), *The Occupation of Japan*, pp. 68–73.

33. Oddly, the government gained control over interest rates only as a consequence of the Antimonopoly Law. In 1947 the Fair Trade Commission ruled that the traditional practice of setting maximum interest rates by interbank agreements was 'collusive' and must be discontinued. SCAP believed that interest rates could not be allowed to float freely in the unsettled and extraordinary economic circumstances and so authorised the Japanese government to set maximum rates for the duration of the inflationary 'emergency'. Thus, this key prerogative fell to the Governor of the Bank of Japan, strengthening governmental controls over finance and hindering the emergence of free-market forces in credit allocation. The temporary arrangement became permanent and, in the years of the economic 'miracle', the bureaucratic control over interest rates was to prove of critical importance in maintaining the 'artificially-low interest rate' policy. Fuji Bank, *Banking in modern Japan*, p. 216.

34. Memorandum, 'Monetary situation in Japan', LeCount to Marquat, 28 January 1949, Dodge Ms., Japan 1949 Box 1.

35. Letter, Dodge to Ikeda Hayato, 9 August 1949, Dodge Ms., Japan 1949 Box 3.

36. Memorandum, Dodge to Marquat, 29 November 1950, Dodge Ms., Japan 1951 Box 1.

37. Letter, Dodge to Marquat, 19 April 1950, Dodge Ms., Japan 1950 Box 3.

38. Memorandum, Dodge to Marquat, 29 November 1950.

39. Memorandum of conversation with Ichimada, by Dodge, 9 November 1951, Dodge Ms., Japan 1951 Box 1.

40. Letter, Dodge to Marquat, 19 April 1950.

41. Quoted in Arthur Woodford, *Detroit and its banks* (Wayne State University Press, Detroit, 1974), p. 181.

42. Letter, Dodge to Marquat, 16 September 1949, Dodge Ms., Japan 1949 Box 2.

43. Memorandum, Dodge to Marquat, 29 November 1950.

44. For example, when Dodge was President of the American Bankers' Association he led a campaign for voluntary reform and credit restraint by the US commercial banks, thus hoping to forestall direct government action. Woodford, *Detroit*, pp. 199–200.

45. Letter, Dodge to Ikeda, 1 February 1950, Dodge Ms., Japan 1950 Box 4.

46. Cable, Dodge to Draper, 21 February 1949, SCAP-WNRC, RG331 Box 539.

47. Kil, 'The Dodge Line', p. 83.

48. Nanto, 'The United States' role', p. 279.

49. Memorandum for record by Dodge, 27 April 1949, Dodge Ms., Japan 1949 Box 9.

50. Letter, Dodge to Ikeda, 9 August 1949.

51. Letter, Dodge to Ikeda, 1 February 1950.

52. Yoshino Toshihiko, 'Economic recovery and the banking system', *Contemporary Japan*, 24 (April 1957), p. 586.

53. *RFB Monthly Report*, June 1949, Dodge Ms., Japan 1949 Box 2.

54. Memorandum of conversation with Ichimada, by Dodge, 1 April 1949, Dodge Ms., Japan 1949 Box 6.

55. Hugh Patrick, *Monetary policy and central banking in contemporary Japan* (University of Bombay Series in Monetary and International Economics no. 5, Bombay, 1962), p. 72. See also Appendix II.

56. Ibid., p. 129.

57. Memorandum, J.R. Allison to Dodge, 27 November 1950, Dodge Ms., Japan 1950 Box 4.

58. Y. Suzuki, 'An analysis on business results of city banks from the Dodge-line policy', *Monthly Circular of the Mitsubishi Economic Research Institute* (March 1953), pp. 8–26.

59. 'Feud between BOJ and Finance Ministry over financial policy', *Japan Review*, 28, no. 15 (17 August 1950).

60. Memorandum of conversation with Ichimada, by Dodge, 9 February 1950, SCAP–WNRC RG331 Box 7691.

61. Memorandum of conversation with representatives of Japanese government, by McDiarmid, 24 March 1949, Dodge Ms., Japan 1949 Box 6. On the basis of the experience in Occupied Germany (which Dodge was, of course, familiar with), the occupiers may well have expected a different reaction from the Policy Board. Following the 1948 currency reform in Germany, the Bank deutscher Lander adopted a strict (and often unpopular) programme of monetary restraint to support price stability and the balance of payments equilibrium. Cf. Wallich, *Mainsprings*, pp. 76–85.

62. This change was significant as, at the time, commercial banks generally lent at the maximum legal rate. Patrick, *Monetary policy*, p. 129.

63. Edna Ehrlich and Frank Tamagna, 'Japan' in Benjamin Beckhart (ed.), *Banking systems* (Columbia University Press, New York, 1954), p. 529.

64. Fuji Bank, *Banking in modern Japan*, p. 203.

65. The increasing power of the Bank of Japan during the Occupation is presented in detail by Calder, 'Politics and the market', pp. 149–52.

66. Memorandum, Dodge to Marquat, 29 November 1950.

67. Adams and Hoshii, *Financial history*, pp. 56–7.

68. The interbank call money market was active and reasonably market-oriented during the Occupation's tenure, yet its existence did little to promote the 'Americanisation' of the Japanese financial system.

69. Letter, Dodge to Marquat, 19 April 1950.

70. Letter, Marquat to Dodge, 13 May 1950, Dodge Ms., Japan 1950 Box 3.

71. Memorandum, Dodge to Marquat, 29 November 1950.

72. Ibid.

73. Ibid.

74. Ibid.

75. Ibid.

76. Memorandum of conversation with Ichimada, by Dodge, 9 February 1950.

77. Suzuki, 'An analysis of business results', pp. 11–12.

78. Conference transcript, Dodge-Ichimada, 30 November 1950, Dodge Ms., Japan 1950 Box 6.

79. Ibid., and memorandum of conversation with Ichimada, by Dodge, 9 November 1951, Dodge Ms., Japan 1951 Box 1.

80. Memorandum, signed J. Smith (ESS–FI), 12 December 1950, SCAP-WNRC, RG331 Box 7502.

81. '13 questions and answers', presented by SCAP to Ambassador Hodgson, Allied Council, March 1950, SCAP-WNRC, RG331 Box 7691.

82. Ibid.

83. Letter, Marquat to Dodge, 13 May 1950.

84. Letter, Dodge to Marquat, 16 June 1950, Dodge Ms., Japan 1950 Box 7.

85. Letter, Dodge to R. Reid, 7 March 1951, Dodge Ms., Japan 1951 Box 2.

86. Conference transcript, Dodge-Ikeda, 25 October 1950, Dodge Ms., Japan 1950 Box 7.

87. Prior to the JDB decision, Dodge had approved the foundation of specialised governmental financial institutions which were presumably 'apolitical' and compatible with US aims: the Peoples' Finance Corporation (1949), which aimed to promote small businesses; the Housing Loan Corporation (1950), designed to support residential construction; the Export Bank of Japan (1950), charged with furthering overseas commerce. The Ministry of Finance apparently hoped to soften Dodge's opposition to government banks by gaining approval for these institutions before proposing the more controversial JDB. These tactics, like the deft handling of the Industrial Bank rehabilitation, proved most successful. Interview with Suzuki Gengo (Liaison Office, Ministry of Finance, 1949–52), 10 April 1986.

88. Kil, 'The Dodge Line', p. 222.

89. Memorandum of meeting on JDB policy, by Dodge, 16 November 1951, Dodge Ms., Japan 1951 Box 1.

90. Johnson, *Japan's public policy companies*, p. 95.

91. Kil, 'The Dodge Line', pp. 227–8.

92. Johnson, *MITI*, pp. 209–10.

93. Ibid., p. 210.

94. Letter, W.W. Diehl to Dodge, 1 June 1951, Dodge Ms., Japan 1951 Box 3.

95. Letter, E.M. Reed (ESS–FI) to Dodge, 20 March 1951, Dodge Ms., Japan 1951 Box 3.

96. Quoted in Cohen, *Japan's postwar economy*, p. 90.

97. Comments by Martin Bronfenbrenner in Redford (ed.), *The Occupation of Japan*, p. 71.

98. Memorandum, Kano Hisakira to Dodge, 12 April 1950, Dodge Ms., Japan 1950 Box 5.

CHAPTER 6

1. It is interesting to note that Ted Cohen's description of the 'trust buster' Corwin Edwards — 'To him, democracy meant freedom of choice, whether of goods, policies or people. He saw the world as a kind of market place' — would apply equally well to Joseph Dodge. Cohen, *Remaking Japan*, p. 355.

2. Robert Ward, 'Conclusion' in Ward and Sakamoto (eds), *Democratizing Japan*, pp. 396-7.

3. Cohen, *Remaking Japan*, p. 381; Cohen also recounted that 'Dodge did not want the SCAP people to brief him. Before he knew anything about Japan's problems at first hand, he was presenting us with his solutions' (p. 431).

4. Walter Bagehot, *Lombard Street*, reprint of 1915 edn (Arno Press, New York, 1978), p. 310.

5. Sakakibara Eisuke and Noguchi Yukio, 'Dissecting the Finance Ministry — Bank of Japan dynasty', *Japan Echo* VI, no. 4 (1977), p. 101.

6. Calder, 'Politics and the market', pp. 280-4.

7. Recent views of the transformation underway in Japanese finance are given by Hamada Koichi and Horiuchi Akiyoshi, 'The political economy of the financial market' in Yamamura Kozo and Yasuba Yasukichi (eds), *The political economy of Japan*, vol. 1 (Stanford University Press, Stanford, 1987), pp. 223-60, and Stephen Bronte, *Japanese finance: markets and institutions* (Euromoney Publications, London, 1982).

Bibliography

ARCHIVAL SOURCES

Joseph M. Dodge Papers. Burton Historical Collection, Detroit Public Library, Detroit, Michigan

National Archives, Record Group 43: Far Eastern Commission — US Delegation Subject Files. Diplomatic Branch, deposited at National Archives Building, Washington DC

National Archives, Record Group 331: Records of Allied Operational and Occupation Headquarters, World War II. Deposited at the Washington National Records Center (WNRC), Suitland, Maryland

National Archives, Record Group 335: Records of the Under Secretary of the Army. Modern Military Branch, deposited at Washington National Records Center, Suitland, Maryland

PUBLIC DOCUMENTS

Japan, Foreign Office (1949) *Documents concerning the Allied Occupation and control of Japan*, vol. III: 'Financial, economic and reparations', Tokyo, August

Japan, Ministry of Finance, Financial Commissioner's Office (1950) *Guide to economic law of Japan*, Kobunsha, Tokyo

Mission on Japanese Combines (1946) *Report, Part 1*, Dept. of State Publication 2628, Far Eastern Series 14, Government Printing Office (GPO), Washington

Supreme Commander for the Allied Powers (SCAP) (1947) *Two years of Occupation: economic*, Public Information Officer, Tokyo

—— (1952) *History of the non-military activities of the Occupation of Japan, 1945–51* SCAP, Tokyo

—— (1970) *Political reorientation of Japan*, 2 volumes, Greenwood Press reprint, Westport, Conn.

United States Board of Governors of the Federal Reserve System (1954) *The Federal Reserve System*, Ralph Young (ed.), Board of Governors, Washington

United States Department of State (1947) *Occupation of Germany: policy and progress, 1945–6*, European Series 23, GPO, Washington, August

—— (1947) *U.S. economic policy toward Germany*, Economic Series 15, GPO, Washington

—— (1950) *Postwar foreign policy preparation, 1939–45*, General Foreign Policy Series 15, GPO, Washington

—— (1950) *A decade of American foreign policy, 1941–49*, prepared for the Senate Subcommittee on Foreign Relations, 81st Congress, GPO, Washington

BOOKS

Adams, T.F.M. and Hoshii Iwao (1972) *A financial history of the new Japan*, Kodansha International, Tokyo

Araki Mitsutaro (1933) *Financial system in Japan*, Japanese Council, Institute of Pacific Relations, Tokyo

Aufricht, Hans (ed.) (1962) *Central bank legislation*, International Monetary Fund, Washington

Backer, John (1971) *Priming the German economy*, Duke University Press, Durham

Bagehot, Walter (1978) *Lombard Street*, reprint of 1915 edn, Arno Press, New York

Ball, W. Macmahon (1948) *Japan . . . enemy or ally?*, Cassell and Co., London

Bank of Japan, Economic Research Department L.S. Pressnell, (ed), S. Nishimura (trans.) (1973) *Money and banking in Japan*, Macmillan, London

—— (1978) *The Japanese financial system*, The Bank of Japan, Tokyo

Bisson, T.A. (1976) *Zaibatsu dissolution in Japan*, Greenwood Press, Westport, Conn.

Bloomfield, Arthur and John Jensen (1951) *Banking reform in South Korea*, Federal Reserve Bank of New York, New York

Borden, William S. (1984) *The Pacific alliance: United States foreign economic policy and Japanese trade recovery, 1947–1955*, University of Wisconsin Press, Madison

Borton, Hugh (1967) *American presurrender planning for postwar Japan*, Occasional Papers of the East Asian Institute, Columbia University, New York

Bronte, Stephen (1982) *Japanese finance: markets and institutions*, Euromoney Publications, London

Clay, Lucius D. (1950) *Decision in Germany*, Heinemann, London

Cohen, Jerome B. (1949) *Japan's economy in the war and reconstruction*, University of Minnesota Press, Minneapolis

—— (1958) *Japan's postwar economy*, Indiana University Press, Bloomington

Cohen, Theodore (1987) Herbert Passin (ed.), *Remaking Japan: the American Occupation as new deal*, Free Press, New York

Dower, John (1979) *Empire and aftermath*, Harvard East Asian Monographs no. 84, Cambridge

Fuji Bank Ltd (1967) *Banking in modern Japan*, 2nd edn, The Fuji Bank, Tokyo

Gayn, Mark (1981) *Japan diary*, Charles Tuttle, Rutland, Vt.

Gimbel, Jack (1968) *The American Occupation of Germany*, Stanford University Press, Stanford

Goldsmith, Raymond (1983) *The financial development of Japan, 1868–1977*, Yale University Press, New Haven

Hadley, Eleanor (1970) *Antitrust in Japan*, Princeton University Press, Princeton

Hirschmeier, Johannes and Yui Tsunehiko (1981) *The development of Japanese business: 1600–1980*, 2nd edn, George Allen and Unwin, London

Hogan, Michael J. (1987) *The Marshall Plan*, Cambridge University Press, Cambridge

Industrial Bank of Japan (1957) *Long-term credit banking system of Japan*, The Industrial Bank, Tokyo

Japanese laws relating to banks (1982) EHS Law Series, vol. VI, nos 6000–9, Eibun Horei-sha, Tokyo

Johnson, Chalmers (1978) *Japan's public policy companies*, American Enterprise Institute, Washington

—— (1982) *MITI and the Japanese miracle*, Stanford University Press, Stanford

Kennan, George F. (1967) *Memoirs, 1925–1950*, Atlantic Monthly Press, Boston

Kindleberger, Charles (1984) *A financial history of Western Europe*, George Allen and Unwin, London

—— (1987) *Marshall plan days*, Allen and Unwin, Boston

Livingston, J., Moore, J. and Oldfather, F. (eds) (1973) *Postwar Japan*, Pantheon, New York

Martin, Edwin M. (1948) *The Allied Occupation of Japan*, Institute of Pacific Relations, New York

Mills, Walter (ed.) (1951) *The Forrestal diaries*, Viking Press, New York

Mitsubishi Economic Research Institute (1936) *Japanese trade and industry: present and future*, Macmillan, London

—— (1955) *Mitsui — Mitsubishi — Sumitomo*, Mitsubishi Economic Research Institute, Tokyo

Mitsui Bank (1976) *A history of the first 100 years*, Mitsui Bank Ltd, Tokyo

Nakamura Takafusa, J. Kaminsky (trans.), (1981) *The postwar Japanese economy*, University of Tokyo Press, Tokyo

—— R.A. Feldman (trans.), (1983) *Economic growth in prewar Japan*, Yale University Press, New Haven

Nolte, Sharon H. (1987) *Liberalism in modern Japan: Ishibashi Tanzan and his teachers, 1905–1960*, University of California Press, Berkeley

Oppler, Alfred C. (1976) *Legal reform in occupied Japan*, Princeton University Press, Princeton

Patrick, Hugh (1962) *Monetary policy and central banking in contemporary Japan*, University of Bombay Series in Monetary and International Economics no. 5, Bombay

Rausch, Basil (1980) *The history of the New Deal, 1933–1938*, 2nd edn, Octagon Books, New York

Rosecrance, R.N. (1962) *Australian diplomacy and Japan, 1945–1951*, Cambridge University Press, London

Sakurai Kinichiro (1964) *Financial aspects of economic development of Japan*, Science Council of Japan, Economic Series 34, Tokyo

Sarasas, Phra (1940) *Money and banking in Japan*, Heath Cranton, London

Schiffer, Hubert F. (1962) *The modern Japanese banking system*, University Publishers, New York

Shonfield, Andrew (1965) *Modern capitalism*, Oxford University Press, for the Royal Institute of International Affairs, London

Spindler, J. Andrew (1984) *The politics of international credit : private finance and foreign policy in Germany and Japan*, Brookings Institution, Washington

Suzuki Yoshio (1980) *Money and banking in contemporary Japan*, Yale University Press, New Haven

Wallich, Henry C. (1955) *Mainsprings of the German revival*, Yale University Press, New Haven

Wildes, Harry Emerson (1954) *Typhoon in Tokyo*, George Allen and Unwin, London

Wilson, J.S.G. (1978) *Industrial banking: a comparative survey*, Société Universitaire Européene de Recherches Financières, Series 18A

—— (1986) *Banking policy and structure*, Croom Helm, London

Woodford, Arthur M. (1974) *Detroit and its banks: the story of Detroit Bank and Trust*, Wayne State University Press, Detroit

Yoshida Shigeru, Yoshida Kenichi (trans.) (1961) *The Yoshida memoirs*, Heinemann, London

Zysman, John (1983) *Governments, markets and growth*, Martin Robertson, Oxford

ARTICLES

Adler, Hans (1949) 'The post-war reorganization of the German banking system', *Quarterly Journal of Economics* LXIII, no. 3, August, pp. 322–41

Asakura Kokichi (1967) 'The characteristics of finance in the Meiji period (the period of take-off)', *The Developing Economies* V, no. 2, June, pp. 274–300

Backer, John (1984) 'From Morgenthau Plan to Marshall Plan' in Robert Wolfe (ed.), *Americans as proconsuls*, Southern Illinois State University Press, Carbondale, pp. 155–65

Beplat, Tristan E. (1980) 'Banking and deconcentration' in Lawrence Redford (ed.), *The Occupation of Japan: economic policy and reform*, The MacArthur Memorial, Norfolk, Virginia, pp. 236–40

Bronfenbrenner, Martin (1950) 'Four positions on Japanese finance', *Journal of Political Economy*, LVIII, no. 4, August, pp. 281–8

—— (1951) 'Economic policy under MacArthur', *United Asia*, vol. 3, no. 4, pp. 249–55

—— (1975) 'Inflation theories of the SCAP period', *History of Political Economy*, vol. 7, no. 2, pp. 137–55

Cho Yukio (1967) 'From the Showa economic crisis to military economy', *The Developing Economies* V, no. 4, December, pp. 568–96

—— (1974) 'Exposing the incompetence of the bourgeoisie: the financial panic of 1927', *Japan Interpreter* 8, no. 4, winter, pp. 492–501

Dower, John (1975) 'Occupied Japan as history and Occupation history as politics', *Journal of Asian Studies* XXXIV, no. 2, February, pp. 485–504

Edwards, Corwin D. (1946) 'The dissolution of the Japanese combines', *Pacific Affairs* XIX, no. 3, September, pp. 227–40

Ehrlich, Edna and Frank Tamagna (1954) 'Japan' in Benjamin Beckhart (ed.), *Banking systems*, Columbia University Press, New York, pp. 517–71

Fine, Sherwood (1952) 'Japan's postwar industrial recovery', *Contemporary Japan* XXI, nos. 4–6, pp. 165–214

Hamada Koichi and Horiuchi Akiyoshi (1987) 'The political economy of the financial market' in Yamamura Kozo and Yasuba Yasukichi (eds), *The political economy of Japan*, vol. 1, Stanford University Press, Stanford, pp. 223–60

Hollerman, Leon (1979) 'International economic controls in Occupied Japan', *Journal of Asian Studies* XXXVIII, no. 4, August, pp. 707–19

Kawaguchi Hiroshi (1967) 'The "dual structure" of finance in post-war Japan', *The Developing Economies* V, no. 2, June, pp. 301–28

Langdon, Frank C. (1961) 'Big business lobbying in Japan: the case of central bank reform', *American Political Science Review* LV, no. 3, September, pp. 527–38

Maier, Charles S. (1981) 'The two postwar eras and the conditions for stability in twentieth century Western Europe', *American Historical Review* 86, no. 2, April, pp. 327–52

Mayo, Marlene (1980) 'American economic planning for Occupied Japan: the issue of *zaibatsu* dissolution' in Redford (ed.), *The Occupation of Japan: economic policy and reform*, pp. 205–28

—— (1984) 'American wartime planning for Occupied Japan: the role of the experts' in Wolfe (ed.), *Americans as proconsuls*, pp. 3–51

McDiarmid, Orville J. (1980) 'The Dodge and Young Missions' in Redford (ed.), *The Occupation of Japan: economic policy and reform*, pp. 59–71

Neuberger, H. and H.H. Stokes (1975) 'German banking and Japanese banking: a comparative analysis', *Journal of Economic History* 35, March, pp. 238–52

Patrick, Hugh (1967) 'Japan, 1868–1914' in Rondo Cameron (ed.), *Banking in the early stages of industrialization*, Oxford University Press, New York, pp. 239–89

—— (1971) 'The economic muddle of the 1920s' in J.W. Morley (ed.), *Dilemmas of growth in prewar Japan*, Princeton University Press, Princeton

Pempel, T.J. (1987) 'The tar baby target: "reform" of the Japanese bureaucracy' in Robert Ward and Sakamoto Yoshikazu (eds), *Democratizing Japan*, University of Hawaii Press, Honolulu, pp. 157–87

Roberts, John G. (1979) 'The "Japan crowd" and the zaibatsu restoration', *Japan Interpreter* 12, nos. 3–4, summer, pp. 384–415

Sakakibara Eisuke and Noguchi Yukio (1977) 'Dissecting the Finance Ministry — Bank of Japan dynasty', *Japan Echo* IV, no. 4, pp. 98–123

Suzuki, Y. (1953) 'An analysis on business results of city banks from the Dodge-line policy', *Monthly Circular of the Mitsubishi Economic Research Organization*, March, pp. 8–26

Takahashi Makoto (1967) 'The development of war-time economic controls', *The Developing Economies* V, no. 4, December, pp. 648–65

Tsuru Shigeto (1949) 'Toward economic stability in Japan', *Pacific Affairs*, vol. 22, December, pp. 357–66

Wikawa Tadao (1929) 'The banking system of Japan' in H.P. Willis and B.H. Beckhart (eds), *Foreign banking systems*, Pitman and Sons, London, pp. 816–68

Yamamura Kozo (1972) 'Japan, 1868–1930: a revised view' in Rondo Cameron (ed.), *Banking and economic development*, Oxford University Press, New York, pp. 168–98

Yoshino Toshihiko (1957) 'Economic recovery and the banking system', *Contemporary Japan* 24, April pp. 570–95

—— (1977) 'The creation of the Bank of Japan — its Western origin and adaptation', *The Developing Economies* XV, no. 3, September, pp. 381–401

UNPUBLISHED DISSERTATIONS

Calder, Kent (1979) 'Politics and the market: the dynamics of Japanese credit allocation, 1946–78', PhD, Harvard University

Ehrlich, Edna (1960) 'The role of banking in Japan's economic development', PhD, The New School for Social Research

Hosoya Masahiro (1982) 'Selected aspects of zaibatsu dissolution in Occupied Japan, 1945–52', PhD, Yale University

Hutchinson, Edward C. (1954) 'Inflation and stabilization in postwar Japan', PhD, University of Virginia

Kil, Soong Hoom (1977) 'The Dodge Line and the Japanese conservative party', PhD, University of Michigan

Nanto, Dick K. (1976) 'The United States' role in the postwar economic recovery of Japan', PhD, Harvard College

Rice, R.B. (1974) 'Hitachi: Japanese industry in an era of militarism, 1937–1945', PhD, Harvard University

Tsutsui, William M. (1985) 'Stabilization and reconstruction in Japan, 1945–1950', A.B. thesis, Harvard College

Index

For Product Safety Concerns and Information please contact our EU representative GPSR@taylorandfrancis.com Taylor & Francis Verlag GmbH, Kaufingerstraße 24, 80331 München, Germany

T - #0142 - 270225 - C0 - 234/156/10 - PB - 9780415852692 - Gloss Lamination